COUNTY DURHAM
FOLK
TALES

COUNTY DURHAM FOLK TALES

ADAM BUSHNELL

The
History
Press

For Sarah

First published 2017

The History Press
The Mill, Brimscombe Port
Stroud, Gloucestershire, GL5 2QG
www.thehistorypress.co.uk

Text © Adam Bushnell, 2017
Illustrations © Nigel Clifton, 2017

British Library Cataloguing in Publication Data.
A catalogue record for this book is available from the British Library.

ISBN 978 0 7509 8150 7

Typesetting and origination by The History Press
Printed and bound by TJ International Ltd, Padstow, Cornwall

CONTENTS

ACKNOWLEDGEMENTS

I thank Chris Bostock who suggested I write the book in the first place. My thanks also go to my parents, my partner, Lorna, Isla and my son, Michael, for all of their help with the project.

Thanks too to Keith and Maggie Bell, the owners of Crook Hall and Anna the supervisor and events manager of the amazing place. Thanks also to my editors from number 7, Harry and Dee.

Huge thanks to Nigel Clifton, the incredible and talented illustrator of this book.

I also want to express my deep thanks and eternal gratitude to Paul Martin, Ian McKone and Dave Silk for all of their fantastic input and assistance. I could not have written this book without them. Cheers lads.

INTRODUCTION

I have always been a storyteller.

I was a teacher and now I run creative writing workshops in schools as a visiting author. I write academic books on writing but my real love is writing fiction. I have been lucky enough to be published several times and I enjoy telling stories through the written word. But I also love to tell stories orally.

I first started working as a storyteller over ten years ago. In this time I have gathered stories from all over the world but it is the stories from my home in County Durham that I adore best of all.

In this collection of my favourite tales I have included the major landmarks of the county: Durham Cathedral, Durham Castle, Hylton Castle, Lumley Castle and more. There are some stunning places to visit here in our county. I would like to think that the book could be used as a visitors' guide to our vast and varied home. Come and see the places where the stories are set. Soak in the spooky atmosphere and grand architecture. Immerse yourself utterly in the narrative, by being in the place where dragons roamed, giants stomped and witches cackled.

Hartlepool, Sunderland and South Shields are now no longer part of County Durham but I have included these locations and some of their stories, as this is a book of *old* County Durham. The old county where worms slithered, vampires hunted and people hung monkeys.

There are some truly horrible tales in the book like the character Andrew Mills, an axe murderer from Ferryhill, and Peg Polwer, a child-eating water witch from Middleton in Teesdale. There are darkly comic tales such as 'The Pickled Parson' from Sedgefield and 'Nicky Nacky Field' from Tudhoe. There are stories of three of the northern saints: Cuthbert, Bede and Godric. There are friendly ghosts such as 'The Ghost of Hylton Castle' from Sunderland and 'Dobbie and Cloggy' from Shotton and Staindrop. Sinister fairies such as 'The Faery in the Quarry' from Middridge and 'The Pensher Hill Fairies' from Penshaw, feature. Old stories such as 'Bishop Auckland Boar' and new stories such as 'The Durham Puma' are included too.

But, ask anyone what he or she believes the most famous story from old County Durham is and the answer is likely to be 'The Lambton Worm'. It is a superb story and, of course, I have included it at the end of the book but there are other less famous stories that are equally interesting and just as exciting. These are the tales that I really wanted to tell. The ones that have almost disappeared, until now. 'A Vampire in South Shields', 'The Soldier in the Wall' and 'The Seer from Cotherstone' to name just three. There's also another 'worm' story that is a classic. 'The Sockburn Worm' tells a tale to rival John Lambton's quest.

The stories are rich and diverse just as the landscape that County Durham offers is too. We have beautiful beaches, incredible woodland, picturesque country villages, bustling towns and breathtaking natural beauty everywhere you look.

This is a book of the familiar and the unfamiliar. They are all brand new re-imaginings of stories rather than simply retellings. I have interpreted them in my own way. I have combined some stories together such as in 'The Grey Lady of Durham Castle' and 'The Giants of County Durham'.

Some of the stories have similar tales from other locations. For example, 'The Fairies from the Cave' is very similar to a story from Rothley Mill near Newcastle.

Some are completely new stories that have been based upon scraps of information after a lot of research, such as 'The High

Green Ghost' and 'The Picktree Brag'. I have created fictional tales based around real life characters such as in 'The Battle of Neville's Cross' and 'Sir John Duck'. But the tales are told to reflect as much factual information about these people and the events as I could find.

I'm originally from Hartlepool and have lived in Durham for over ten years. I'm passionate about my home. I'm passionate about the place and I'm passionate about the people. But, I think I'm even more passionate about the stories that are all around this beautiful county.

So, prepare to step into a world of witches, ghosts, dragons, spirits, murderers, knights, giants and fairies ...

> Whisht! Lads, haad yor gobs,
> An Aa'll tell ye's aall some *awesome stories*
> Whisht! Lads, haad yor gobs,
> An' Aa'll tell ye *more than just the worm*!

Adam Bushnell
2017

1

SIR JOHN DUCK

Young John arrived at the brow of a hill. The view that greeted him took his breath away. A silver river coiled the city like a warm embrace. In the very centre were the most beautiful buildings he had ever seen in his life. It was the incredible Durham Cathedral and it was sat next to an astonishing castle.

He sighed long and loud.

'This will be my home,' he breathed, 'This will be my city.'

John had apprenticed as a butcher and was now ready to make it on his own. His plan was to get a job in the city and eventually have his own shop. He had dreamt of it his whole life.

He almost skipped towards a bridge and then went on into the centre towards the market square. He stood on Silver Street and gasped again. The market was the busiest, most bustling place he had ever seen in his life. Market traders, mainly butchers, had stalls set up everywhere. His feet squelched as he stepped forward. He looked down and saw the cobblestones running red with blood. The metallic tang of the blood was all around as he neared the stalls. Vast wooden chopping boards with heavy cleavers displayed huge joints of mutton, beef, lamb, veal, rabbit, grouse; all manner of meat. There were fishmongers too. The stench of the fish entwined with the heavy scent of the raw meat. It made John's head swim. Then there were big bundles of dried herbs to mask the tidal waves of smells but they didn't work. John didn't mind though. He could not keep the smile from his face as he walked from stall to stall. It was tattooed there. A permanent toothy grin.

'Excuse me, sir!' he called cheerfully to one butcher, 'Do you need any help?'

'Ya wha?' the burly man barked back.

He was red-faced and had a blood-encrusted leather apron over a perfect sphere of a belly.

'I've done my apprenticeship!' John replied, 'I can butcher!'

'Where'd ya train? Which stall? Why've they got rid of ya?'

'Oh, I'm not from Durham.'

'Not from Durham?' laughed the man meanly, 'Then forget it. Ya won't work round here unless ya *from* here!'

'Really? Why?'

But the man had turned his back on him and was busy carving pigs' trotters.

John tried anther stall and was given the same response.

Then another. And another.

The butchers of Durham would only hire those trained in Durham.

'You need to belong to our guild,' explained one butcher who was a little friendlier than the others, 'We only take on Durham Guild butchers. It's been that way since 1402 and that's that.'

'But how do I join your guild?' John asked.

'If you got your apprenticeship outside of the guild then you can never join the guild. Sorry!'

John kicked at the cobblestones in frustration. All of his dreams were dashed in the city he had yearned for.

Slowly, he trudged his way back to the bridge and away from the market square.

His attention was firmly fixed at his feet but a squawking made him look up. Circling above him was a black raven. John shrugged and continued his long journey home. But the raven squawked again.

'Shoo!' called John, 'I'm not a dead man yet!'

John hurried his pace and the raven followed. Eventually he stopped and peered up at the large bird. It seemed to be holding

something in its claws. Now that John
had stopped, the raven swooped
down and landed at his feet. It
dropped whatever it had been cra-
dling and with a noisy scoop of air
in wings, then flapped away.

Stepping forward, then crouch-
ing, John peered at what the raven had left him. It was a silver coin
on the cobbles of the street that led to Silver Street.

The boy picked it up and bit it to see if it was real. It was! He
smiled. At least some good had come out of the day. This would
see him have a warm meal and a comfortable night in the city, then
it would be back home the next day with change to spare.

Just then he heard puffing, panting and cursing. A man was
struggling to move two cows.

'Damn you, you stubborn pair!' the man raged.

'Are you going to sell those?' asked John.

'I was!' the man spat, 'I've been trying to get them to the market
all day long but the beasts won't move!'

'I'll buy them!' the boy said at once, 'Here!' He held out the coin
to the man.

'I'd have liked more for them,' he said slowly, 'But enough is
enough. They're yours and good luck to you!'

The man snatched the coin from the boy's hand and scurried
away up the road.

John stroked the snouts of the cows. He talked to them kindly
and softly. When he tugged at their harnesses, the cows happily
walked on. Leading them back the way he had come, to the market
square, the boy's smile was back.

'How much do you want for those cows?' The voice came louder
than the rest of the hubbub of noise.

John's smile was wider than ever.

'Who's asking?' he called back to the crowd.

One man stepped forward. It was the first burly butcher he'd
spoken to earlier.

'I am,' he barked back at the boy, 'Oh, it's you!'

'It is!' beamed John, 'How much are you offering?'

'Don't trade with him!' another man said, stepping in between the two, 'He'll rob you blind!'

'Oh yeah?' said the first burly man.

The two men began arguing.

'I don't care who I trade with, I just want an honest price!'

'Then talk to me!'

Another man stepped forward. This third man extended a hand for John to shake.

'I'm John,' smiled the man.

'So am I!' laughed the boy.

'John Heslop.'

'John Duck!'

'Pleased to meet you,'

'Likewise!'

John Heslop bought the cows from John Duck. He was so impressed by the boy's cheerful demeanour and enthusiastic attitude that he hired him as an apprentice, despite the protests of the Durham's Guild of Butchers. The boy did end up owning his own butcher's, but he ended up with a lot more too. He continued to trade on the market square. He was a wise buyer.

He bought and sold first beasts for farms then, at last, the farms themselves. He made shrewd investments in land and soon became known right across the County of Durham. He built himself a fine mansion in Haswell, where he lived with his wife, the daughter of John Heslop.

He eventually became the Mayor of Durham and rose to the rank of a baronet when he became Sir John Duck of Haswell on the Hill.

John never forgot the raven that helped him though. He decided that he wanted to give something back to the city that had looked after him. So, with his wealth, he built a hospital in Great Lumley for the poor and needy.

The boy without a penny to his name will always be remembered in the county as the man who rose to greatness in his beloved city. There is a pub that bears his name on Claypath that leads to Silver Street. The logo beside the name is a raven holding a coin. It stands on the place where the boy first began to make his fortune.

2

THE FAIRIES FROM THE CAVE

Fairy Hole Cave sits between Eastgate and Westgate in Weardale, near to Killhope Lead Mining Museum. It is a deep cave with a long history. It is also the home to fairies.

A boy lived at a mill near to Cowshill. He was mean and nasty to all he met. He was cruel and vicious. He laughed at the unfortunate. He was also very lonely.

The boy used to collect stones to keep in his pocket. He would walk through the woods and throw these stones at squirrels and birds. He would pick flowers only to tear them to pieces. He would trample ferns and shred leaves. In short, he would take out his loneliness on anything he could.

One bright autumn morning, the boy was walking near the woods when he came across a small limekiln. The fires had long since cooled so the boy climbed on top of the tower of stones. It had a turfed roof. He peered inside from the grassy top. He decided that this would be an excellent vantage point to launch stones at passing rabbits. Heaping the pile of rocky missiles to his side, he then lay back upon the soft grass and decided to have a snooze.

A tinkling sound that sang in the distance soon interrupted his sleeping. He sat up. It was quite unlike any other sound that he had heard before. It was a ringing that danced over the hills and, quite involuntarily, made him smile from ear to ear. He squeezed his eyelids together, squinting over the green landscape to see the source of the sound.

There was a whole procession of fairy folk. Each would have been no higher than the boy's kneecap. They came dancing and singing along the land. Some carried hurdy-gurdies, turning the handles and tapping at the keys. Some played pipes, some played fiddles, some sang, some danced. They all made up a merry band and the boy flipped himself over onto his stomach. He became perfectly still. He held his breath. He was scared. He had never seen fairies before. Of course, he had heard of them, but he had always thought that the boys and girls from his village were making up stories. He had been convinced that there was no such thing. He had said it often enough and given those same children a firm punch for making up lies. Yet, here they were. Fairy folk in the flesh.

The boy slid his eyes over to the pile of stones next to him. A cruel smile slithered over his mouth. The fairies continued their merry parading dance until they got to the base of the kiln. Then the music came to an abrupt halt. The echo of it drifted on the air like a whisper of smoke.

Each fairy was wearing the colours of an autumnal landscape – reds, browns, yellows, all beautifully decorated with leaf and branch patterns. Their hair was plaited and their eyes were shining. They chatted and laughed. Their voices were high-pitched, singsong and musical. Busying themselves by unloading leather backpacks, the fairies were completely oblivious to the boy's presence above them. He was a still statue atop the stones.

Once the musical instruments were safely stored away, the fairy folk unpacked small sticks and kindling. They entered the kiln and busied themselves preparing a fire within. Daring to move merely a matter of inches, the boy peered down the long shaft of the kiln to see what was happening within. He felt smoke upon his cheeks. Floating, grey wafts came gently drifting from little orange flames. A cooking pot was being hoisted onto a metal tripod over the fire. Water was poured from small leather pouches and then herbs were added. One fairy was delightedly adding great handfuls of honey.

'Sweet tea,' he giggled, 'Honey makes it sweet!'

The others laughed and encouraged him to add more. Their voices mingled with the smoke and the boy beamed. But his smile was not like that of the fairies. His smile was a cruel and taunting thing. He slithered his arm over the grass until he could feel the hard stones against his fingers. He slid them closer to the opening of the kiln. Then he waited, like an ancient spider.

The fairies were stirring the heavily scented tea with a large wooden spoon. Some were sat in a circle around a fire, some had taken up their instruments again and were playing slow, melancholic tunes while others stared into the now large flames.

Several minutes passed and the boy remained still and silent. The fairies had passed around acorn cups and were all busy sipping their herbal tea. The taste of honey was in the air and the boy licked his lips. He inched himself forward, very slowly and very quietly.

Gripping a stone in each hand, he aimed carefully. The fairies were utterly oblivious to the boy above. He dropped both stones, which landed perfectly into the pit over the fire. Boiling tea splashed in every direction, soaking the shocked fairies. The boy rolled onto his back and exploded with laughter. Rolling back again, he looked down into the kiln. The shocked fairy folk were up on their feet; the acorn cups fell to the ground. They rubbed at themselves gasping in surprise.

The boy laughed and pointed at them.

The fairies looked up at their attacker. Their faces instantly changed. The eyes that had previously shone with laughter and music narrowed. Their expressions, once filled with kindness, now bore rage. Arched eyebrows framed fury.

'Burn and scald.' one fairy said, 'Burn and scald.'

The fairies all pointed up at the boy at exactly the same time.

'Burn and scald,' others joined in, 'Burn and scald.'

Laughter soon stopped from above the kiln. The boy saw and heard the fairies and became frightened. He sat up on his knees.

'Burn and scald!' All the fairies now chanted together. 'Burn and scald!'

The boy was now up on his feet. He scurried away from the kiln top as fast as he could. The fairies had emerged from the kiln entrance though. Their voices a shriek upon the wind.

'Burn and scald!' They pointed at the fleeing boy, 'Burn and scald!'

He kept looking over his shoulder and fell to the floor. He landed with a soft thump. He turned and saw the fairies running over the grass towards him.

'Burn and scald! Burn and scald!'

Jumping back to his feet, the boy cried out in terror as the mass of fairies tore across the landscape. His foot fell into a rabbit hole and the boy tumbled to the floor again.

'Burn and scald! Burn and scald!'

The fairies were almost upon him. He lunged forward. He felt the scratching of fingers on his legs. They were upon him. He had to be fast.

'Burn and scald! Burn and scald!'

The firm fingers found soft flesh. The fairies gripped the boy's legs and he sank to the ground once more. Then they were climbing over him, scratching and tearing at his leg.

'Burn and scald! Burn and scald!'

The boy kicked wildly and managed to get back upon his feet. He raced over the grass and did not look back. He sprinted to a cluster of trees. He could not hear the fairies. He turned and could not see them either. He hunched himself over, breathless and panting.

'Stupid fairies,' he said at last. Standing up to his full height he looked back at the kiln.

'They didn't scare me.'

That night, sleep did not come easily for the boy. He turned in his bed this way and that. His mind was buzzing with memories of fairies that stung. The boy did at last fall into a fitful sleep. But, in the middle of the night, a terrible pain in his leg awaked him. It was the leg that the fairies had scratched and torn at.

He bolted up and flung the covers to the floor. The pain was terrible. It was a burning pain. A scalding pain.

He pulled up his pyjamas and saw that his leg was blackened and scorched. He tried to cry out in anguish but the pain had taken his voice. Wild, wide eyes gulped in the scene. His leg was withered. He would never walk again.

'I'm sorry,' he gasped at last, 'I'm sorry! I'll never hurt anyone or anything again!'

With those words his leg was healed. The flesh returned to its normal colour. The pain was gone. He fell back onto the bed and breathed out long and hard.

The next morning, the boy was out in the woods. He saw a squirrel scamper up a trunk of a tree. He grinned and found a stone in his pocket. But as he went to pick it up his leg burned. The stone fell to the floor and the pain went away.

Later, as he went to strip a young tree of its leaves, that same scalding pain returned.

The boy nodded. He stared at his leg. At last he understood. The fairies had left their mark upon him forever and he would never be the same. It was not a mark visible to anyone else. It was a mark inside of him. He looked from the trees towards the kiln in the distance. Beyond that he saw the mouth of a cave. The boy smiled. He was changed. For the better.

3

THE SOCKBURN WORM

The River Tees coils and snakes its way around the North East of England. The serpentine river fuels High Force Waterfall, not far from its source, and slithers east, past Barnard Castle, continues to travel near to Darlington and finds its way into the North Sea once it has past Stockton and Middlesbrough. It can be seen from the Bowes Museum, Preston Park Museum and Grounds, Durham Tees Valley Airport and Middlesbrough's Riverside Stadium. It invades both counties of Yorkshire and Durham. But it is at the southernmost point on this river's journey that it surrounds a place known as Sockburn. This was a land said to have been plagued by a terrible dragon. The creature was known as a 'worm'. This name came from the Anglo Saxon word for dragon, which was 'wyrm', and also the Germanic word, also for dragon, which was 'wurm'. The Sockburn Worm was a legless dragon that coiled and snaked across the land just as the River Tees still does today. It could breath poisonous gas that filled the air with deadly toxins on each exhalation. This meant that no living soul could even get near it, let alone fight it. It fed on cattle mainly, but also on people.

When Sockburn was known as Storkburn, the manor house did not yet belong to the Conyers family. It was the youngest son of the Conyers, whose name was John, who got the idea into his head that it should be he that killed the creature.

'I've had enough!' bellowed a farmer. 'It's already eaten my entire flock of sheep! How am I meant to make a living?'

This was met by much nodding and mumbling.

'We're cursed!' added the tanner. 'That's what we are! We must have done something! This worm is a plague sent by God to punish us!'

Some agreed. Plenty didn't.

John Conyers sat and listened. He heard the people of Storkburn. He was just a small page, not even a squire, but he had big plans and even bigger ideas.

He raced to the castle where his father was talking to his knights.

'The people of Storkburn call upon us!' His father boomed, his voice authoritative and theatrical, 'We must kill this monstrous creature.'

The knights dared to glance at one another but none of them uttered a word. John nodded and smiled. His father was a brave man and an excellent leader. Perhaps it would not be young John who would defeat the worm but his father. He would lead his knights into battle and defeat this monstrous worm.

'We have found its lair. It lives beneath the ground at the foot of a hill. At Graystone. It sleeps as we speak. There isn't a moment to lose. Summon your squires. We are leaving within the hour.'

The knights were clearly shocked by the sudden news but all moved as one into action.

There was clanging and rattling as armour was strapped onto gambesons. Helms were donned and weapons strapped to belts. War hammers, swords, maces, axes and spears were all gleaming with anticipation. The horses were readied and Lord Conyers bellowed commands.

Hooves clattered onto cobblestones as the small army rode off towards the deadly creature. John Conyers ran after them. He watched them gallop into the distance, following the trail of muddy hoof prints upon the land.

Soon they were a cloud of dust in the distance. Then the dust settled and John's burning legs slowed from a sprint to a jog and now to slow walk. He so desperately wanted to see the battle but knew it would all be over by the time he got there. He imagined his father holding aloft the head of the slain beast with a triumphant smile upon his face. There would be feasting and celebrating for days. The people would be happy once more. His father would be a hero. John's chest heaved with pride.

Once his breath had returned and his muscles regained their strength, he was off running again. He turned the corner to the hill and abruptly stopped at Graystone. A thick fog curled and slithered over the land and John could make out only shapes. Shapes of people. Of horses. There were bodies everywhere. Limbs lay scattered. Blood pooled all over. The whole army had been torn apart.

John raced into the cold, harsh embrace of the swirling fog. His eyes darted across each mangled victim until at last he saw his own father. Lifeless eyes stared out of wide sockets. The skin had a green tinge to it, visible even through the dense blanket of fog. Thin, blue veins clawed at the cheeks. The mouth was open, wide and twisted as if the last moments of life were experienced in excruciating pain. The toxic gas from the worm's breath had killed them all. John knelt bedside his father and tears rolled silently down his cheeks.

Hearing a low rumbling, he looked up to see a large, scaled tail sliding beneath the earth into a huge hole in the ground. The worm.

John felt rage rising within him. His hands shook. He stood on unsteady legs and a ghastly stench filled his nostrils. The bitter, acrid taste of poison was still in the air.

Dragging his heavily armoured father over the land and out of the lair of the worm, he thought hard about what he, a mere page, a small boy, could do to defeat this dragon. He coughed and choked. After only managing to make it a few feet away from the site of devastation, John knew that he couldn't do this alone. This army of knights had stood no chance. His father had been too reckless. John saw this clearly through the mist and the death. If he were to avenge his father's death and save the land he loved, he would need help.

He dropped his father's lifeless limbs and turned away.

There was only one person who could help him. An old woman who lived by herself on the riverbank. Some called her a witch, others called her Wiccan, but all referred to her as wise. She was the wise woman of the Tees. She knew a great many forgotten things. She knew the ways of the past. She knew of monsters and how to stop them.

The boy was running again. He was running away from the horrible scene. He was running towards the one person who could make him a hero. The one person who could help him avenge his father's murder.

The wise woman lived in a small cottage. Tendrils of smoke coiled from the chimney. John knew she was at home. He hammered at the door, heaving a lungful of air. The door was opened abruptly. Tear-streaked cheeks and desperate eyes stared up at the face in the doorframe.

'You'd better come in,' she croaked.

John nodded, panting and stepped inside. Once his eyes had adjusted to the darkness of the cottage he looked around. Bookshelves lined the walls holding countless dusty volumes. But there were also jars of strange objects pickled to preserve them: snakes, lizards, frogs, toads, even brains that looked large enough to be human. There were maps, scrolls, papyrus, parchments and letters everywhere. Bottles of liquids adorned the top of each shelf. Dried herbs of a startling variety hung from the wooden beams. A vast fireplace with a huge cauldron dominated the scene.

The woman gestured a gnarled and twisted claw of hand towards a three-legged stool next to the fire.

'Sit on the cracket,' she nodded at the stool.

John did as instructed.

'We'll have a bit of crack on the cracket, eh?'

The boy nodded slightly.

'Tell me your woe and I'll make it all go,' she smiled.

Her teeth were not in plentiful supply. Tufts of grey hair sprouted from her chin. White hair surrounded her head in sparse wisps. Yet, despite her appearance, she gave John a calming feeling. She seemed to ooze kindness and wisdom all at once. He sighed and told her what he had seen.

She shook her head slowly.

'Things like dragons have always been,' she croaked. 'They always will be. But this one has grown too wicked. It has allowed greed and lust to overrun itself. It must be stopped.'

She began nodding now.

'You must be the one. You must slay the worm.'

John was nodding too.

'I know,' he heard himself say, 'I've always known, I suppose.'

She raised a bushy, grey eyebrow.

'I mean, I dreamt this. When I was very young,' he explained. 'I dreamt I killed a dragon.'

She nodded again.

'You'll need this then!'

She stood up and hobbled over to a large wooden chest at the other side of the room. Mumbling to herself, she pulled free a tabard, a buckler and then a pair of gauntlets.

'No, no, no.' she muttered. 'Not those. None of those.'

At last a large helmet was produced. She held it aloft like some prized trophy she had just won.

'Here it is!'

She limped back over to the fire. The orange light glinted on the old helmet. It was spotted with patches of very dark rust.

'It's a great helm,' she said handing out the helmet to John.

He took it and gasped at the weight.

'It's heavy.'

She nodded.

'It's old.' she said as if giving an explanation for its weight.

There was a cross made of metal on the front. The horizontal line of the cross opened into an eye slit. Clusters of holes were either side of the vertical one of the cross.

'Wear that,' the old woman ordered, 'and no poisonous gas can harm you.'

John turned it this way and that. He could feel the power in it.

'There's more though,' the old woman said and went back to the cavernous chest.

The boy sat, transfixed. The wise woman began muttering again as she rifled through the treasure trove of a chest.

She whirled around holding a sword. It was a long blade that was mainly straight but ended with a large curve at the tip.

'This is a falchion,' she said stepping back towards the fire. 'When I'm done with it, it will be able to cut through anything.'

John put down the heavy helmet and watched in awe as the old woman thrust the blade into the fire. The orange flames licked at the silver metal and seemed to intensify. The fire flashed a yellow colour and the old woman withdrew the weapon. She then took a handful of dried rowan leaves and sprinkled these along the length of the blade. It was then returned to the now orange fire. The dried leaves crackled and fizzed and popped.

She then pushed the sword in further and let go. The handle was wobbling uncertainly.

'Go on then,' smiled the old woman. 'Make it yours.'

John nodded and stood up. He grabbed the handle and pulled free the sword from the flames.

'Kill the worm.'

With the helmet in one hand the sword in the other, John strode towards the door. He turned and looked at the wise woman.

'Thank you.'

He then slipped through the door and walked towards Graystone. The fog had now gone, revealing the gory sight even more clearly. His father lay upon his back with the same deathly gaze staring up at the sun.

John pulled down the helmet and walked past the dead with the sword gripped firmly in his hand he approached the hole in the ground.

He thought he might have to lure the creature out, but as soon as he began to think how he might do this, the ground began to shake. It was a deep, low rumbling at first but then rocks bounced and soil rolled aside.

The worm burst forth from the hole and reared up into the air. Its tail was still below ground but its head roared at the boy. A black tongue spat venom at the floor. Rows of snarling yellow teeth drooled thick translucent saliva. Red and black slitted eyes burned with fury. They were fixated on the boy before it.

The worm slithered onto the floor and moved in an S shape along the floor. It was now fully out of the hole and hissed noisily as it approached.

John shifted his weight from one foot to another; back and forth he went, readying himself to strike when the worm was close enough.

Then the dragon reared up onto its tail again. It let forth a blast of air from its deadly mouth. A dense cloud of green vapour engulfed John. He could not see for a few moments. The worm hissed noisily again, as if satisfied with its efforts.

The helmet worked. John was alive.

The worm seemed confused for a few moments then lunged again to unleash more of its toxic breath.

John noticed that when it let out its deadly gas, the creature closed its eyes. That was all he needed. While the worm was blinded by its own breath, John raced forward and hacked at its neck with the falchion. Black blood burst in a vast wave. It landed noisily onto the boy with sickening sounds.

The worm roared, more out of surprise than anger. John hacked again near to the first wound. This attack did not wound so deeply. The dragon let out another burst of poisonous gas and John plunged the blade up to the hilt. He turned the sword first one way and then another. The worm let out gurgling sounds. It was stunned. Its eyes widened in shock. The black tongue lolled to one side.

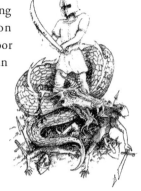

John pulled free the sword and using both hands he slashed down upon the neck. The dragon fell to the floor and spat black blood repeatedly. John hacked again and again. Soon the head came free from the neck. The thick, gloopy blood ran like syrup being poured from a tin.

The body slumped to the floor. John still held the sword in both hands; his head rocked forward and the massive helmet fell from his head onto the floor with a soft thud. He looked over to his father.

'I did it,' he breathed heavily and quietly.

He strapped the sword to his side and put the helmet onto a large and vicious-looking horn on the worm's head. The boy then staggered back to the castle dragging the huge head by the other horn.

It took an age, but eventually he made it. The farmers in their fields saw him first. Then the word spread across the whole of Storkburn. Here was John Conyers, the slayer of dragons. The boy dropped to his knees and held the sword to the sky.

The falchion, the sword that slew the worm, can still be seen to this day. It hangs in Durham Cathedral in their Open Treasure collection.

The sword's fame spread. All knew John Conyers' story. The story still lives on and takes on a new life of its own. It is a story that continues to inspire authors across the ages. Lewis Carroll wrote 'The Jabberwocky' after hearing it. Perhaps it will inspire you too. Perhaps you will do great things as the young page did in this tale.

Sockburn, – where Conyers so trusty
A huge serpent did dish up,
That had else eat the Bish-up,
But now his old faulchion's grown rusty, grown rusty.

from The Bishopprick Garland

4

VENERABLE BEDE

Bede was born near the River Wear in Sunderland in AD 672. He lived nearly all of his life in a monastery in Jarrow and rests in a tomb in Durham Cathedral. He was a monk who wrote over sixty books in his lifetime including the first book of English history, which he completed in AD 731.

Bede wrote all of his own work by hand. He said that he was his own secretary as he dictated, composed and copied his work all by himself. But when the monk was 62 years old he finally relented and asked for a young monk called Wilbert to be his scribe. All of those years working in dim candlelight had finally got the better of the monk. Bede's eyes were failing and he could longer write. He would have to dictate his translation of St John's Gospel. He was working on an Anglo Saxon version of the gospel as many did not understand Greek or Latin.

He still loved to walk through the fields and paths down to the River Wear. It was a path he could walk without sight. There, he would sit and listen to the birdsong and the splashing of the river on the rocks. He would close his eyes and feel close to the natural world that he loved so much.

It was when he was sitting and listening to nature that a young boy came running along the riverbank. When he saw the old monk, the mischievous boy smiled. He wanted to play a trick on

Bede. He stopped and thought for a few moments then chuckled to himself.

He raced over to the monk, shouting,

'Father!' he called, 'Father! There's a group of people who have travelled for miles to hear your wise words!'

Bede opened his eyes and sat up straight.

'They've come for a sermon?' he asked.

'They arrived too late for this morning's preaching and want to hear you now!' the boy went on.

The monk stood up, shakily.

'They've sent me to fetch you! They want you to preach in the fields!'

Bede nodded.

'Guide me there, young man.' he said. 'My eyes aren't what they were, so you can lead the way.'

The boy stifled his laughter and skipped over to take Bede's arm. He led the old monk over towards a field of wild flowers and long grass.

'Do you see them, Father?' the boy asked. 'Do you see the people?'

All Bede could make out were blurry shapes in the distance. He assumed that this was the crowd that had gathered for him.

'This is your congregation, Father,' the boy went on in a whisper. 'They are silent out of respect for you.'

Bede smiled and ruffled the boy's hair. The old monk stepped forward towards the trees, grass and flowers with his arms raised.

'Welcome,' he said. 'Welcome to you all.'

He then knelt on the ground and said a prayer. When he stood up he began to give his sermon. Bede spoke of the wonders of the world. He told the story of creation. He explained the seasons, the tides, the orbiting of the Earth around the sun and the orbiting of the moon. He linked everything to God's perfect design.

All the while, the boy rolled around in the grass laughing and guffawing. He tried to be as quiet as he could but the sight of the old monk preaching to plants was just too amusing to not laugh out loud.

'What a stupid old goat he is,' the boy said to himself, 'When he's finished, I'll tell him what he's done. He'll feel like the fool he really is. Everyone thinks he's so amazing. This'll teach him. This'll make him see that the old are useless.'

The boy chuckled as he imagined the monk's embarrassment.

Meanwhile, Bede continued his sermon and talked of the life of Jesus. He explained how we could all be like Him and love one another, forgive one another and teach one another. He likened this way of life to nature; that this too was all God's perfect design.

When Bede came to the end of his sermon, he again got down onto his knees to pray to God.

As he did so, the air was filled with a myriad of voice that all chorused the same thing.

'Amen, Venerable Bede. Amen, Venerable Bede.'

The voices were clear and as one but seemed to be coming from every direction.

The boy stopped laughing and stood up. He turned this way and that. He tried to see who was speaking. Were there people hiding in the grass? Lurking in the bushes? Sitting in the trees?

'Amen, Venerable Bede. Amen, Venerable Bede.'

There were no people. It was the grass that was speaking. It was the bushes and the trees. It was nature itself that commended Bede on his sermon.

'Amen, Venerable Bede. Amen, Venerable Bede.'

The boy opened and closed his mouth. He had no words. He could not speak. He walked over to the monk and put his hand on the kneeling man's shoulder.

'Amen, Venerable Bede. Amen,' said the boy.

Bede stood up and smiled at him.

The boy's cheeks flushed with shame. He knew that the word venerable meant that it was someone who should be given a great deal of respect because of his or her age and wisdom. It was a word that fitted the monk perfectly.

He took Bede's hand and led him back to the monastery. On the way, the boy told the monk of the cruel trick he had played and what had then happened. Bede just smiled and told the boy that it was all right. He told the boy that he had been young once too.

When they arrived at the monastery the boy told the monks the story. He also told the story when he returned home. He told the story to anyone and everyone. He told it to so many people that the name Venerable Bede is one that people still use today for the old monk from Sunderland.

5

THE SEER FROM COTHERSTONE

Lord Fitz-Heugh loved to hunt. He would often be seen tracking foxes, baiting hares and pursuing boars. But it was the red deer of the Teesdale that he most loved to hunt. He would blast his horn and race through the forests at impossible speeds. He would only hunt alone as no other could keep up with him. He was so skilled a huntsman that stories of his prowess were known far and wide across the whole county.

It was one fine summer's day when Lord Fitz-Heugh was trotting down a long lane towards Cotherstone. He was looking forward to tracking a herd of deer he had heard lived close by. It was the mighty stag he was after.

The sun blazed upon him and he smiled. Its warm embrace was welcoming and his smile broadened as he heard the light splashing of the River Tees nearby. The aroma of wild flowers mixed with the fresh morning air and Lord Fitz-Heugh sat atop his saddle for a few moments breathing in the heavily scented air. He closed his eyes and savoured the feeling.

'Pardon me, my lord,' croaked a voice from below, 'I don't mean to disturb you.'

Lord Fitz-Heugh snapped his eyes open and as they adjusted to the bright light he squinted at the figure beside his horse. It was a very old and very wrinkled old woman. She had thick, slate grey hair tied back into a rough ponytail. One eye bulged larger than the other yet sparkled a brilliant blue. She smiled up at him, revealing just one large tooth set upon pink gums. Wisps of thick grey hairs protruded from her chin.

'My dear lady,' the lord smiled. 'Are you well?'

'Indeed I am,' the old woman smiled.

Lord Fitz-Heugh slipped down from his saddle landing with a heavy thump upon the path.

'Can I help you?' he asked. 'Do you need a ride home?'

'No, it is you I seek.'

'Me?' asked the startled lord. 'But why?'

The old woman stared at the lord directly for a few moments. Lord Fitz-Heugh's gaze was transfixed upon the mysterious lady.

'Beware of Percy Myre Rock,' she said firmly. 'Do not go there today. Avoid the crag and avoid your doom!'

A befuddled expression fell upon the lord's face. Percy Myre Rock was right beside Cotherstone and certainly on his hunting ground for the day.

'How do you know such a thing?' asked the bewildered lord.

'The older I get, the further I see,' the woman said in hushed tones. She almost whispered the words then shook her head, smiling.

'As my eyesight fades, I see more clearly.'

Lord Fitz-Heugh just stared at her.

'If you go to Percy Myre Rock today then the Fitz-Heugh line ends with you,' she went on. 'Fate needs more of your family in this world. Your family line will do great good in this land. But that means that you need to continue that line.'

She paused in order to let her words sink in.

'Heed my warning and live,' she said at last. 'Ignore my words and die today.'

It seemed to the lord that she had finished her premonition. He smiled at her.

'I thank you,' he smiled and nodded, 'and I appreciate the advice.'

He then turned from her to his saddlebag.

'Here, let me offer you a little something by way of thanking you.'

He turned back and held out a coin.

But she had gone.

'Strange,' he said aloud.

He peered first one way up the lane and then the other. It simply was not possible that one so old could move so swiftly. He would have heard her entering the undergrowth of the forest either side of the lane. She had simply vanished.

Now, Lord Fitz-Heugh was not a superstitious man. He generally dismissed such premonitions and warnings as stuff and nonsense. But there was something in the way that the old woman had spoken that had made him listen.

He would hunt on this side of the river to thus avoid Percy Myre Rock on the other side.

For the whole day, the lord tracked the herd of deer but he found no sign of them. Then, later in the afternoon, he saw them gathered on the other side of the water. He cursed and trotted beside the riverbank staring out at the deer.

'I'll cross the river,' he said to himself, 'but I'll stay away from the crag.'

He nodded briskly. He was not in the habit of talking aloud to himself yet had done so twice since his encounter with the old woman. He knew it to be foolish. He knew he was simply justifying his own actions by saying them out loud. He was not a man to second-guess himself ordinarily.

Finding a shallow path over the river, Lord Fitz-Heugh guided his horse to the other side. He stayed down wind of the deer and cautiously approached them. The silent hooves of the horse crept through the woods towards a clearing where the deer grazed.

It was then that Lord Fitz-Heugh saw the most magnificent stag he had ever seen in his life. It towered above the other deer with a proud and heavily antlered head. Its smooth sleek skin seemed to glow red in the late afternoon sunlight.

He flicked the reins and his horse softly stepped forward towards the magnificent beast. A twig snapped. All at once, the herd of deer turned their heads as one. Lord Fitz-Heugh remained frozen in his saddle but with an explosion of movement the deer fled away from him. Their thunderous galloping made the lord exclaim as he kicked his spurs upon his horse. He had to have that stag. No matter what, it would be his.

The horse burst onto the clearing and gave chase. The pursuit led him away from the river. Lord Fitz-Heugh was so transfixed upon his prey that he did not notice the creeping darkness as dusk approached. He did not notice the long shadows merging into one another. Nor did he notice the dim light that was slowly fading.

He tore towards the stag. He saw only the charging heels of the stag fleeing at great speed. He saw it ascending a green slope. Lord Fitz-Heugh was right on top of the stag when he saw it leap over the edge of the crag and come crashing down on the other side.

The words of the old woman raced through his mind, as he pulled hard at the reins.

'Halt!' he screamed.

But it was all too late. The horse leaped blindly after the stag and plunged over the edge of the crag. The crumpled stag lay broken and dead at the bottom of the jagged rocks. Its tongue lolled to one side and red blood ran freely over the yellow stone.

This was the last sight Lord Fitz-Heugh saw as he and his horse fell to their deaths beside the fallen stag at Percy Myre Rock.

What great good would the lord have done if he had lived? No one will ever know.

6

THE DEVIL'S BOY

Brass House Farm near Ferryhill is the site of a most terrible tale. On a cold January night in 1683 the devil spoke to Andrew Mills and told him to kill. He obeyed and murdered three children in their beds with an axe.

Be warned. This is not a tale for the faint hearted …

Jane Brass laughed.

'They'll be fine!' she said soothingly. 'I'll keep an eye on them both.'

John and Margaret looked at each other, then they both smiled.

'You're a good girl, Jane,' John said and gave her a hug.

'These Christmas parties are never ending!' Margaret said, shaking her head. 'We're up to our eyes until Candlemas!'

'Go!' Jane laughed again. 'Have fun!'

Her parents went off to get ready. Jane went to check on her brother John and sister Elizabeth. They were playing together near the fire.

It was already dark out and the servant boy Andrew was feeding the oxen and putting the chickens into their coops. He was a strange boy who followed her around a lot but he was harmless enough. She watched him from the window of the farmhouse.

'Right, we're off,' said her father as he walked down the stairs. 'It won't be a late one.'

'Give me a hug!' called Margaret.

John and Elizabeth raced to their mother and hugged her. Then they were back by the fire playing their games once more.

'See,' said Jane, 'they're fine. Now go!'

Jane then knelt by the fire and joined in with their games. Jane was 16, John was 12 and Elizabeth was 10.

After locking their children safely in the house, John and Margaret waved to Andrew the servant boy.

'Go home, Andrew!' John called. 'It's late!'

The pair then turned up their collars and headed down the lane towards Ferryhill. Andrew watched them go. He nodded. It was late and he was tired. He slowly walked to the cowshed and slid the bolt across to lock the cows in for the night.

It was at this moment that two voices spoke simultaneously inside his head.

'Kill all!' they said.

Andrew turned to see who had spoken the dreadful words.

'Kill all!'

It was a command. It came from inside his own head.

'Kill all!'

Andrew's eyes slid over to the farmhouse. He could see the orange glow of the fire. He could just about make out the laughter from within.

The boy then walked over to the tool shed. He scanned the contents. His gaze finally rested upon a large felling axe.

An empty smile grew upon his face. He took the axe and made his way towards the house.

Andrew tried the handle of the front door. It was locked. He banged at the door with the axe.

'What do you want, Andrew?' Jane called through the wood.

He didn't reply. He knocked again.

'It's locked and my parents have the key,' she shouted. 'What do you want?'

She peered through the window beside the door at him.

He held up the axe and shouted back,

'Kill all!'

Jane screamed. She turned and ran into the living room. She grabbed her siblings and raced up the stairs. They flew into Elizabeth's bedroom and bolted the door shut.

Andrew began to swing the axe. The huge blade tore hungrily through the wood of the door. With every swing and slam the Brass children cried out in terror.

Andrew stepped into the kitchen. He grabbed a large kitchen knife and stuffed it into his belt behind him. Dragging the axe noisily across the floor, he slowly and deliberately stomped up the stairs.

The axe smashed into the bedroom door and, in two more heavy hits, it flew from its hinges.

Jane rushed forward with her hands outstretched.

'Please, Andrew!' she sobbed. 'No!'

He pushed the girl onto the floor.

John jumped up and lunged his fists at Andrew but the axe-wielding servant boy hit him on the head. John slumped to the floor and then Andrew cut his throat with the blade of the axe. Jane screamed as she watched the blood flow. Andrew pushed the boy aside and stepped towards Jane. She screamed again. The axe came thudding down and she was silent.

Elizabeth was hiding under the sheets sobbing loudly. Andrew pulled them off her. He stared down at the crying girl.

'Please Andrew, don't,' she begged. 'Remember all of those times we played with my dolls? We chased the ducks, remember?'

The boy stopped. His eyes darted between the axe and the girl.

'Do you remember when we chased the ducks?'

Andrew turned and walked out of the room. He stood and looked down the corridor.

That was when he saw it. The devil appeared to Andrew in the form of a hideous creature. It had the head of a wolf, legs of a stag and body of an eagle. The monstrous wings flapped three times then circled the boy. Fiery red eyes glowed as it stared at him:

> Go back, thou hateful wretch, resume thy cursed knife,
> I long to view more blood, spare not the young one's life.'

Andrew turned away from the apparition and walked slowly back into the bedroom.

With a heavy thud he dropped the bloody axe. He took the kitchen knife in his hand and stepped towards the bed. Elizabeth was the third victim that night.

Andrew ran down the stairs leaving the axe and knife in the bedroom. He was covered in blood from head to toe.

He ran from the farmhouse and into Ferryhill. There he heard the bustling party from a grand mansion. He hammered at the door. When it was answered, Andrew pushed his way into the party. The stunned onlookers fell silent.

'Two men broke into your house,' he blurted out, pointing at the Brass parents. 'They killed your children and shouted "Kill all!" as they did it! I heard them!'

There was silence again.

Then Margaret stepped forward and pointed at Andrew.

'Villain,' she spat, 'none other but you have killed my children!'

The guests then fell upon Andrew and dragged him to some troopers who were staying at Ferryhill. They had been on their way from Darlington to Durham and happened to be spending the night there. Andrew was arrested and eventually convicted of his crimes. He told the court that the devil had made him do it.

He was returned to Ferryhill for the execution. His arms and legs were tied with chains and he was bound in an iron cage. The cage was set out overlooking the farmhouse where the murders had occurred. That way, Andrew's last sight would be the horrific scene of the crime.

He did not die quickly. His howls of pain and torment were heard in Ferryhill and beyond. Ravens devoured his eyes first then his flesh. Eventually when the screams of torment were no more and he was dead, the body was left in the cage to decompose. Finally he was cut down and burned. His ashes were blown away over the farmland.

The Brass children were buried in a churchyard in Kirk Merrington.

On the tomb these words are carved:

Reader, remember, sleeping
We were slain;
And here we sleep till we must
Rise again.
Who so sheddeth man's blood, by man shall
His blood be shed.
Thou shalt do no murder.

Andrew Mills, the axe murderer from Ferryhill, can still be heard howling in rage on cold January nights. His ghost is said to be waiting to take his revenge on the people of Durham who killed him.

7

NICKY NACKY FIELD

The reaping had been done. It was time to celebrate. All of the reaping men were invited to the farmer's house in Tudhoe. There were ales and spirits aplenty for all. Nicholas the farmer had been pleased with the work of the men.

'Drink up, fellows!' he roared cheerfully. 'The ale is on me!'

Now this was the first time that Nicholas had invited the reaping men to his home for a drink. Inviting them to 'drink up' was an expensive request. Soon all of the ale and nearly all of the spirits were gone.

'Is there any more?' asked George. 'Is that it?'

Nicolas flushed red with embarrassment.

'Well, lads,' he smiled, 'you've drank me dry. So I guess I'll bid you a good night!'

'What?!' the great roar went up.

'You call that hospitality?' said one reaper.

'The night is young!' added another.

'I thought we were invited here for a good drink!' a third put in.

The farmer shook his head.

'By, you're an expensive lot!' he laughed. 'Tell you what, I'll put in a share of money but you have to contribute too. Let's get some more!'

'Fair enough,' came one reply.

'Aye go on then.'

'I'm not going though.'

With this last statement, a few glances were exchanged.

'Well, I'm not going either,' Nicholas said firmly. 'It's my house.'

A few nodded. A few grumbled. They all looked upon one another. Just then, Walter walked in from using the outhouse.

'Walter!' the entire group called as one.

Walter stood there and opened and closed his mouth a few times. He was usually the butt of their jokes. He could never find the words to join in with their banter. He would often think of replies that he could have given to comments or jokes but they always came to him hours later. Now, here he was, the focus of their attention, yet they were all smiling and being friendly.

'Erm, hullo,' he said awkwardly.

He lifted a hand and did a little wave.

George stepped forward and put an arm around Walter.

'You know that Nicholas here has been very hospitable,' George said in soothing tones as he looked at all of the grinning faces. 'You know we probably owe him a favour.'

Walter nodded slowly.

'Well, we need to replay his kindness.'

Walter nodded again.

'You know we've always liked you the best, don't you?'

Walter did not nod this time.

'Really?' he asked.

'Oh yeah,' smiled George, 'we need the best of us to go on a mission!'

'A mission, you say?'

'We need you to go to the brewery and get us some ale!'

Walter rolled his eyes.

'Oh, no!' he moaned. 'I don't want to go!'

'Just cut through the field yonder,' Nicholas suggested, draining the last of his tankard. 'It won't take long.'

'Nicky Nacky field?' gasped Walter. 'I'm not going through that … it's haunted!'

The reapers fell about laughing.

'It is!' Walter protested, 'That's where it gets its name! It's the noise the ghost makes when he chases you! Nicky, nacky! Nicky, nacky!'

Everyone laughed again.

After a little more protesting, Walter was pushed out into the cold and dark. He shook his head, wrapped a cloak around himself and set off to get the ale.

Meanwhile, inside the farmhouse the spirits were drained and they sat and waited for his return.

They waited.

They waited some more.

At last, they began grumbling.

'Its only a mile or so!' complained George, 'Where is he?'

'It's been hours!'

'Why did we send that fool?'

Just then George stood up. He had a mischievous grin upon his face.

'I know what to do,' he said slyly. 'We'll teach him a lesson for keeping us waiting for ale.'

The reapers chuckled. They knew of George's fondness for practical jokes, especially on Walter.

'What do you propose?' asked Nicholas.

'Have you a plain white bed sheet I can borrow?'

George could barely keep the glee from his face.

'Aye,' nodded Nicholas, 'I do.'

'Well fetch it!'

Once the bed sheet had been brought, George revealed his plan.

'I'll wait in the field for the fool. I'll hide in some of the long grass wrapped in this sheet. When Walter comes walking past I'll give him some "whoos" and "boos" and scare him half to death!'

The farmhouse went up in rapturous applause and laughter.

'A ghost in the field!' laughed George. 'That'll teach him to believe in nonsense.'

So George went off to the field with the sheet under his arm.

Nicholas and the reapers talked about what would happen. They laughed and joked. Then, as before, they waited.

They waited some more.

Then the grumbling started again.

'Where's George got to?'

'It's been hours!'

'I'm going home soon.'

Just then there was a banging and rustling from outside. Walter burst in through the door with a look of horror upon his face. His complexion was ashen and sunken.

'What's the matter, Walter?' asked a reaper, barely stifling a grin. 'You look like you've seen a ghost!'

There were sniggers and chuckles.

'I have!' Walter blurted.

The farmhouse erupted into guffawing laughter.

'In fact, I saw two!' he added.

The reapers were then quiet.

'What do you mean?' asked Nicholas.

'I was on my way back from the brewery, which was closed, by the way.'

There was grumbling.

'When suddenly I saw a white ghost that moaned and howled at me. I was so frightened!'

The reapers nodded, smiling.

'Then another ghost appeared behind the white ghost. It was covered in blacks rags that flapped in the wind. I could only just see it in the moonlight.'

'What did you do?' Nicholas said urgently.

'I said, "Black Ghost ... get the White Ghost!" and he did! The Black Ghost flew up into the air and shrieked like a banshee. The White Ghost yelped and ran but the Black Ghost swooped down and grabbed the White Ghost, all the while making that nicky nacky sound I told you about. Nicky! Nacky! Nicky! Nack!

'Then it flew away, so I ran! All I could hear were bloodcurdling screams and shouts. Then I came here!'

The room fell silent as everyone pondered Walter's words.

They waited for George all night.

Finally, as the dim light of morning crept across the sky, the reapers went off to the field to search for their friend. But all they could find were a few shreds of white bed sheet flecked with spots of blood.

The field is still called the Nicky Nacky Field and the stream that flows past it, and all the way to the Wear, is called Nicky Nack Beck. The Nicky Nack Bridge Inn stood next to the beck. A landlord bought it, renovated and renamed it the Daleside Arms. It was when he did this that he sadly died.

8

THE BISHOP AUCKLAND BOAR

Pollard was bored. He sat in his bedroom and looked at the sun setting across the autumn landscape. Hues of oranges, browns and reds blurred together. Shafts of bright light shone like torches through the trees beyond. Their branches grabbed uselessly at the liquid golden light.

The smell of nettle soup wafted up the stairs. He groaned inwardly. Soup. Again. It had been nothing but boring nettle soup and boring sitting in his bedroom since the curfew was imposed. It was dull. It was monotonous. It was boring and it was all down to a boar.

The attacks had been kept within the wild woods. Hunters had been the first victims. Those who made their living spending long days among dark trees. The trappers, trackers and traders of meat and fur. First one victim was found, mauled to death by tusks and trotters. It happened sometimes. A hunter would stumble upon a sounder of boars. The males would defend their group, the females would defend their offspring. Accidents happened.

But then another victim was found. Then another. And another. All killed in the same way. All had been experts in their trade. None should have been so unlucky. Certainly the likelihood of all four victims making the same stupid mistake was impossible.

Then a fifth was found in the streets that overlooked the woods. That made it a town attack. A man killed by an animal and right there in the town of Bishop Auckland. It was outrageous. News spread quicker than gossip.

The Prince Bishop decided that a full investigation should be made. In the meantime it was a curfew from dusk each and every night. During the day no one should travel the streets alone. Lookouts were posted at the edge of the woods. The boar would be caught and killed. There would be a feast in the very streets it endangered.

But that had been weeks ago. No sightings of the boar had been made. Yet, still, more victims were found. Unlucky travellers, beggars and vagrants all killed in the same way. All had their throats gouged out by unimaginably large tusks, their ragged clothing soaked in their own crimson blood.

The children of the town made up their own tales. Each story became more elaborate until at last each was convinced that the boar was the size of a shire horse, with razor-sharp spines covering the body, trotters made of iron, eyes flaming red and tusks like scimitars.

Pollard pondered this. It was certainly an exciting description, but deep down he knew it simply wasn't true. It was just a big pig. A boar gone mad and rogue. He sighed. When would the thing be caught?

Boastful hunters filled the taverns and reassured the locals that it would be them that brought down the boar. But no one had succeeded. Fewer and fewer arrived in the town to take up the challenge. The Prince Bishop posted fewer lookouts. It was simply accepted that indoors was safe and outdoors was not.

Well, Pollard was still bored. Sitting upon his windowsill he rolled his eyes. He had had enough. He lost himself in fantasies of him bringing down the boar single-handed. He closed his eyes and sighed contentedly at the thought. Imagine the fame, the fortune, the glory; his name would live on in that town forever.

Pollard's eyes snapped open at a sound from below. A snuffling sound. A snorting sound. He peered down through smeared, dirty and warped glass. An involuntary gasp escaped him. He slammed both hands over his mouth. With eyes wide and goosebumps prickling his skin he stared in amazement at the sight below.

A boar, a very big boar, was trotting along past his house. It stopped occasionally to whiff at the air. It stamped and snorted as if proclaiming that this was his town. Then, noisily, it wandered slowly off away from the house and into the woods beyond.

Pollard still clasped his hands over his mouth and watched breathlessly. He stayed like this for some time. Darkness crept towards him. It enveloped him. He had seen the boar! Would he tell his friends? Should he tell his family?

Sleep did not arrive that night. Pollard lay awake lost in a myriad of thoughts. When the morning light crept across the ceiling fighting the shadows back to their sources, he had a plan. He uttered not one word to a living soul of his discovery. The memory of it though was a constant companion throughout the day.

When finally it was time for curfew Pollard could barely contain his excitement. He thundered up the stairs and threw himself against the blurry window of his room with an oomph. His eyes shone with excitement as he scanned the street outside. He waited with bubbling anticipation. He waited until he thought that he would surely burst. Then it came. The boar arrived at the same time and same place as the evening before. It made its snorting proclamations then trotted off into the exact part of the woods that it had done the night before.

'That's where it sleeps,' Pollard whispered in hushed tones to himself.

A smile crept around the edges of his lips. Eventually a full-blown grin was there etched upon his face. It stayed there all of that night and throughout the next day. His mind raced with possibilities and plans. His family and friends asked him what made him so happy but Pollard kept his precious secret tightly locked away, for now.

His only confidant was the dusk that he now welcomed. His smile broadened and he had to stifle a giggle as, for a third night, the boar made its evening rounds. This time Pollard was ready. He had stolen the largest meat knife from the kitchen. His family would not miss it. Soup made from the nettles in their garden was the only food they had eaten for weeks. As the boar trotted away, he made his move. Slipping as quietly as a stealthy fox he descended the stairs. After many nights of raiding kitchen cupboards and the chilling pantry, he was an expert at avoiding the creaks in the wood. His back was against the front door. He peered up the stairs. His family went to bed earlier and earlier each night. Hunger demanded early nights and quick sleep from them.

Turning, he silently lifted the latch and slipped through a slim gap. Following the deep tracks the boar had made in the soft earth, he crouched low as he walked. He just made out the flicking tail disappearing into the woods beyond in the dimming light.

He sighed with relief. His path was downwind of the boar. His scent would be undetectable. He just had to be quiet.

The woods engulfed him. The air became cooler. Bracken crunched beneath his feet, making him stop. He cursed. He had to be lighter of foot. Darkness crept in from every side. What dim light remained was fading fast. There. He made out a groove in the leaf-encrusted floor. The heavy boar had laid a path as clear as the road to the castle. Snapped branches and broken boughs of trees pointed the way.

Pollard grinned. He followed the path with all the patience of an old spider. The boar was in his web. He gripped the knife in his right hand. In the clearing, he saw a huge pit lined with soft ferns, dry grass and patches of moss. This was the boar's pit. The boar was lying on its side in the centre.

Pollard crouched low. Rhythmic breathing filled the air. A deep, snorting and heavy thing.

He stepped forward. One careful step at a time. It took an age. But, finally he arrived at the heart of the pit. The soft lining made for a silent approach. The vast belly of the boar rose and fell like the tide of the sea.

In the last of the light, Pollard made out the beating of a heart. He had to make his aim true and fast. One deep stab in just the right place should do it. Sweat ran down his brow. His mouth was dry and parched. He pulled the knife backward in slow motion. One swift lunge and it would be done. His heart pounded in the silent woodland.

A shrill noise suddenly pierced the air. The boar lifted itself onto its massive trotters at impossible speed for one so large. Pollard stumbled backward and dropped the knife. The head of the boar snorted and roared with fury at the invader that was in its home. The slight glow of a horned moon dripped a little light onto glowing eyes and saliva-dripping tusks.

The boy scuttled backwards like a crab, trying to escape the boar pit. Roaring again, the boar charged. Pollard flung himself to one side. He was still in the pit and the boar frothed from its mouth. It charged again and Pollard leapt out of its path with only a slither of space between him and the mighty, furious beast. He scrambled up and up and up. At last he was free from the pit.

But the boar leapt after him. It thundered its way at him like some possessed demon fleeing from hell. Pollard rolled this way and that. The boar was relentless though. It threw itself at the boy again and again and again.

Then, it started to slow. Its tongue lolled from its cavernous mouth. It was tiring.

Pollard saw his chance. He cajoled the boar. He ran at it, then away again making the creature surge with fury and charge once more. Pollard was small and fast. The beastly boar was not. Finally, after what seemed like hours, the boar slumped down. Breathless and panting, it staggered and fell sideways back into its pit.

Pollard peered at the creature. It still wore an expression of pure anger but it was utterly exhausted. He spied the knife glinting in the slight moonlight. Rocking on his heels, uncertain what to do, he continued to stare first at the boar and then at the knife. Fight or flight? His mind bounced back and forth.

Then, without quite making up his mind to do so, he leapt into the pit. The boar lifted its weary head and snorted a warning. But, undeterred, Pollard scooped up the knife and plunged it into the beating heart. The blade sank into the soft flesh until the boy's hands were scratched by the rough fur. The boar let out a shrill scream. Pollard lifted the knife free and blood splashed his clothes. He stabbed again and again. The boar shrieked and squawked, then fell silent.

Pollard fell backwards, still holding the bloody knife. His chest heaved. His mouth gasped for air. He had done it! The boar was dead.

He felt sleep grip every part of his body. His eyes were laden with weights. Blinking slowly, he breathed out long and hard.

But what if someone would claim his prize as he slept? He knew hunters still occasionally searched the woods for prey at night. One of them could snatch the boar away as he slumbered.

He heaved himself onto an elbow and crawled towards the grisly head. The lolling tongue of the boar was flopped forward. Pollard grabbed it. He sawed and cut, and finally the tongue was loose. It looked like some thick red snake in the slight light. Flinging the knife to one side and stuffing the tongue into his tunic, Pollard then slumped backwards and let sleep take him. He had passed out into a deep, exhausted sleep in seconds.

It just so happened that the boy had been right. A hunter was scouring the woods for skittish rabbits and sleeping pigeons to snare and trap. This hunter could not believe his good fortune when he saw the famous boar dead before him. It must have killed this boy first though.

'No, not dead,' the hunter muttered out loud, 'but sleeping. Bad luck for him!'

He stifled a smile and unfurled a long, thick rope from his belt. Silently and efficiently, the hunter wound coils around the boar's back feet. He then hauled the weighty boar out of the pit. The ground crunched and snapped as the boar slid. The hunter became red faced and groaned under the strain of it. Still, Pollard slept on.

The hunter made it out of the forest and, with a vast amount of effort, hauled the dead boar onto the back of a wagon. Then he was off, with a horse heaving the wagon, up the road towards the castle of the Prince Bishop to collect his reward for delivering the dreaded boar.

When Pollard awoke the first rays of the morning sun were warming his cheeks. He groaned as aching muscles cried out with the effort of merely sitting up.

'My boar!'

He stood.

'My boar!'

Pollard knew almost at once what must have happened. He exploded through the forest following the vast tunnel through the undergrowth made by the dragged boar. Clouds of dust rose beneath his feet as he thundered along the road towards the castle.

'I must see the Prince Bishop,' he declared, panting upon arrival. 'I need to tell him about the boar!'

The guards laughed.

'He already knows!' said one.

'We all do! The beast is dead.' added another.

Pollard pushed past them and entered the throne room. The guards didn't stop him. They laughed again. What harm could it be if this boy witnessed the boar slayer being rewarded for his hard work?

The Prince Bishop was standing before the hunter, counting out golden coins from a leather pouch onto a long wooden table.

'Stop!' bellowed Pollard. 'He didn't kill the boar! I did!'

The entire throne room exploded into laughter. The Prince Bishop raised a hand for silence.

'Really?' he replied with a wry smile. 'And I suppose you have proof to support this claim?'

Pollard stepped defiantly forward.

'Indeed I do!'

The Prince Bishop raised one eyebrow.

'Look inside the boar's mouth!'

All eyes moved as one towards the boar's head.

'Go on!' challenged Pollard. 'Look inside! See if it's missing anything!'

The Prince Bishop looked from Pollard to the hunter to the boar.

'Do it.' he nodded.

Several guards crowded around the boar and one lifted the snout while another held open the bottom jaw.

'It's missing its tongue!' gasped the Prince Bishop.

'It certainly is!' laughed Pollard. 'If he killed the boar then where is the tongue?'

All eyes fell upon the hunter, who shifted uncomfortably under the enquiring looks.

Pollard stepped forward and pulled the tongue free from his tunic.

'I have it! As I killed it!'

He held the gruesome trophy aloft for all to see.

A mighty cheer went up into the throne room. The hunter took this as an opportunity to slip away undetected but was grabbed by a guard.

'Take him away,' ordered the Prince Bishop. 'Lies have consequences.'

Pollard slammed the tongue onto the long wooden table.

'As for you,' smiled the bishop at the boy, 'the reward is now yours.'

Another cheer filled the vast room.

'What is your name?'

'Pollard, sir.'

'Well, Pollard,' smiled the Prince Bishop, 'I like you. In fact, as well as this reward, I'll offer you something else.'

He then turned and sat upon his throne. The anticipation was tangible. Everyone knew the Prince Bishop was a man who loved his entertainment. He liked to play his little games.

'I shall have my breakfast. You may take a horse from the stable. Any land that you have ridden around while I am eating will be yours. You may claim it and call it your own.'

He clapped his hands.

'Guards! Saddle a horse for young Pollard.'

Pollard did not need telling twice. To have his own land and be given the golden coins would transform his and his family's lives forever. He raced off to the stables.

The Prince Bishop laughed and went off to the banquet room to eat. But the bishop was only a few mouthfuls into his morning feast when Pollard returned.

'That was fast!' declared the Prince Bishop, 'Surely you need more time! You'd not like more land?'

Pollard shook his head, smiling.

'No,' he grinned.

'Well, where have you been?' asked the confused bishop.

'I've been for a ride around your castle.'

'What do you mean?'

'You said I could have any land that I rode around while you ate.'

Pollard let his words sink in.

'This castle is now mine then, isn't it?'

The confused bishop opened and closed his mouth a few times.

'Well?' asked Pollard.

'Well I suppose it is, yes!' laughed the Prince Bishop. 'By St Cuthbert! You have got the better of me, as you got the better of the dreadful boar! I'll tell you what. Walk with me.'

The bishop took Pollard outside the castle. They stood and looked across the landscape.

'If I may stay in my own home,' began the Prince Bishop, 'then all of this shall be yours. Agreed?'

Pollard laughed and nodded. The small hill near the palace and all the land surrounding it became known as Pollard's land. To this day, in Etherley Lane in Bishop Auckland, there stands a public house named 'The Pollard's Inn' to remember the boy that bettered the boar … and the bishop.

9

A Vampire in South Shields

James was a baker who lived near the railway in South Shields. A new bakery had opened just next to Mile End Road at the station and business was bad for James.

'There's no loyalty any more,' he grumbled as he stared into the bread kiln. 'No one has any decency.'

His stomach churned as he writhed in his frustration and anger.

'We're meant to be a *community*.'

He stood. Then sat, then stood again.

'We're meant to look out for each other.'

Wearing a dark and foul expression he kicked a stool and stormed up the street towards the railway station. James stood at the corner and peered round at the bustling new bakery. His aquiline nose sneered at the customers to-ing and fro-ing. His peculiarly arched nostrils breathed in deeply.

'Sweet and cinnamon,' he hissed. 'What's wrong with just baking *bread*.'

The bushy eyebrows that framed his dark eyes furrowed. He suddenly heard footsteps behind him and whirled around to see two small boys skipping up the road towards the bakers.

'Look,' whispered one, 'it's him.'

'Look at his pointy ears!' the other laughed back in hushed tones. 'He's like the fairy folk.'

James's face reddened as he roared at the pair and lunged at them with his fingers twisted into claws.

The boys screamed and ran away back up the road. James turned his attention back to the new bakery. Wrapping his arms tightly around himself he raged inwardly.

So began James' new routine. He would light his fires and bake a little bread that he would not sell to anyone. Then he would stand on the street corner and fester in his fury. This was repeated day after day. Occasionally more boys would whisper about him. They would stare and point. They would jeer and laugh. Mostly, he ignored them. Other times he would roar at them or hiss at them or chase them.

One dark and brooding day that matched James's mood perfectly well, he changed his routine. He could take it no more and marched up to the bakery. He pushed past the long line of customers going in and out of the busy bakers.

'I was here first!' he bellowed as he stepped inside. 'These are my customers!'

The shocked patrons turned as one to look at James. His face was flushed red, his eyes were wild and his breathing rasped.

'You're all going to pay!' he screamed hysterically, pointing at each person's face in turn. 'Every last one of you! You'll see! You'll pay!' He turned over a whole shelf of baked rolls and stormed out of the bakery.

There was momentary silence then the shop was instantly filled with noise.

'He's not right!'

'Who does he think he is?'

'What do you suppose he meant?'

'My children say he's not of this earth.'

And so it went. James's outburst was met with rumours and suspicion.

Meanwhile the enraged baker went back to his own bakery and stared into the softly fading embers of his fire. His heavy panting soon slowed into rhythmic deep breathing. He closed his eyes and decided what he wanted to do.

The next morning, it was busy business as usual near Mile End Road. The trains steamed in and out of the station. The customers filed in and out of the bakery. People went about their normal routines. James was not missed. Talk of his rant in the bakery soon disappeared and he was forgotten about entirely as the days went by. That is, until some children were passing the old baker's on their way home. It was the terrible smell that roused their curiosity. They peered in through a dirty window to see the source of the stench. Upon the floor was the body of the baker.

The children screamed and ran in multiple directions to their homes. Soon a small crowd gathered, all peering in at the dead figure of James upon the floor of his bakery. The door was kicked in and a gush of air filled with decomposing flesh fell upon the crowd.

'He's been dead for days,' an old woman said from behind a muffled handkerchief. 'He's gone off!'

'Bit like his bread then!'

This was met with stifled laughter, but it soon died down as the crowd saw the sight before them.

James was lying inside a circular pool of his own blood. He had cut his wrists with a large knife that lay by his side, glistening in the dim light. With the blood drained from his body his complexion was utterly white. Blank, black eyes stared up at the ceiling. His jaw hung to one side revealing rows of small, yellowed teeth.

'A suicide,' said one man shaking his head and making the sign of the cross upon his chest.

'What if he comes back?' a boy asked.

'What do you mean?' asked his mother.

'What if he comes back for some blood for his body?'

Everyone exchanged glances.

'I've heard of this,' said the priest, as he stepped inside the grim bakery. 'Stories from Newborough, Melrose and Alnwick.'

All eyes were upon the priest. More made signs of the cross.

'They date back to the early 1100s,' the priest continued. 'It's a disease of the blood. It makes suicides come back to drink the blood of others. It's called vampirism.'

A gasp escaped the shocked crowd.

'He must be buried on unconsecrated ground,' the priest went on. 'Tonight, at the stroke of midnight. He must also have a wooden stake driven through his heart to keep him in the ground. This alone will stop the creature coming back.'

There was nodding and mumbling.

'Put the body in a coffin,' the priest said to two men. 'Take him to the field over by the station.'

The two men nodded and went off to get a coffin from the coffin maker.

'But that's where we play,' a boy complained. 'On that field is where we meet.'

The priest mumbled something gruffly and walked away.

That night, the same crowd and many more gathered at the field. A deep grave had been dug and they all stood around it. Their faces were gloomy and shadows danced upon them from the orange light of the lanterns.

'Here they come,' a woman commented.

There were four men carrying the coffin upon their shoulders. Behind them were six more men. They seemed to be holding something heavy.

'What's that they carry?' asked the priest.

Upon the coffin was a long wooden pole. It was immensely long, around 30ft in total.

'We've got the stake!' one of then men called.

'And this!' another held aloft a sledgehammer.

'I just meant a small wooden stake for his heart!' said the incredulous priest.

'I know,' another man butted in, 'but we want to make sure he *stays* under ground.'

There was a lot of nodding and mumbling.

'Very well,' relented the priest. 'Do it.'

As the church bells rang out at the stroke of midnight, the lidless coffin was lowered into the deep earth. The vast wooden pole was driven through the body, through the wood below and far into the earth.

Everyone with shovels buried James the vampire baker. There was still 15ft of pole sticking out of the ground when they were finished.

'Where will we play now?' the children asked each other.

'Here,' said the priest firmly. 'You will still play here. Dance and play around the pole. It will keep the body beneath the ground.'

So the children of South Shields kept their playground. They danced around the pole that jutted from the earth to stop the poor baker James from drinking their blood to sustain his own lifeless body.

10

THE PICKTREE BRAG

Bewick was walking back home to Chester le Street. He was exhausted. It had been a long walk to the farm to sell his donkey. Now he had a few coins in his pocket but nothing to ease the ache he felt in his feet. His toes poked through holes. Water seeped inside. He was miserable. He was down on his luck.

Just then, in the distance, he saw something. He stopped and rubbed his eyes. It looked to be a horse, but no, it was too small for a horse, it was a pony.

The curious man stepped towards it and the pony did not shy away or seem to be frightened in any way. Bewick held out a hand. The pony took a few steps forward and first sniffed then licked the hand. The pony was a chestnut colour with deep hazel eyes. The mane was luxuriously thick and longer than any that Bewick had seen before. He ruffled it and the pony whinnied. It was a light, throaty noise.

'Where's your master?' asked Bewick.

The pony snorted, shook his mane then munched at the grass by its hooves.

'I'll take care of you for now,' smiled the man. 'Just until we find your owner. We can't have you out here now, can we?'

Crouching its neck lower, as if inviting the man to climb upon his back, the pony tapped the floor. Bewick smiled. He climbed up onto the pony's back and grabbed two fistfuls of mane. He was about to flick the mane as a gesture to walk on but suddenly the pony thundered into action. It galloped full pelt across the land, slamming hoof after hoof into the soft, marshy floor.

There was a pond ahead.

'Slow down!' screamed Bewick. 'Nooooo!'

The pony looked as if it was going to plunge into the green water but at the last second, it stopped, steadfast on the edge of the pond sending Bewick tumbling into the water.

He landed with a heavy splash and the pony reared up onto its back legs. Bewick looked up from the dank water and it seemed to him that the pony was laughing. Not neighing, nor snorting but an actual laugh. A *human* laugh.

Struggling from the web like reeds of the pond, he finally slumped onto the soft grass.

'Curse you, creature!' he said, getting to his feet.

Just then the pony stopped laughing and stared at Bewick, hard. There was defiance in its eyes. Then all at once it began to change.

The pony reared up onto two legs again but stayed there standing, like a man. The long nose began to retreat into its head, fur fell from its body, hooves turned to hands. Bewick was terrified but also unable to move; he was paralysed with fear as he watched the transmogrification take place.

The ears fell flat, the mane tumbled to the floor and disappeared. The pony changed into a man with no head. It stood there motionless for a few moments and then began to convulse and shake.

With a flow of blood like lava erupting from a volcano, a head began to emerge from the stump. It was accompanied by fingers. A boy climbed out of the body of the man. The headless man's body fell to the floor and the boy oozed himself out of the fleshy encasing.

The boy had a mischievous grin. He stared at Bewick and pointed at him menacingly. Then blood began to pour from the boy's eyes like tears. They ran in straight tracks and dripped onto the floor.

Bewick screamed and ran. He ran and didn't stop running. He was running so fast that he nearly knocked over his neighbour, Henry, in the street.

'What ever is wrong?' asked Henry. 'You look like you've seen the devil himself!'

Hysterically, Bewick told his story. Henry soothed and calmed the man. They sat and talked but Bewick eventually said that he just wanted to go home to sleep. The next day, Henry went to check on his neighbour and found him hanging from his neck in his living room, quite dead.

At Bewick's wake Henry called the whole of the congregation together and told them the tale that he had been told.

'So that is why our friend and neighbour is dead!' Henry declared. 'It is the brag from Picktree.'

'I saw him as a calf!' said a woman, 'It had a white handkerchief around its neck and made a terrible noise. It was a whining cry that would wake the dead!'

'My old mother swears she saw it as fox,' added a man. 'It had a red scarf and led a whole pack of hounds into the pond.'

'Well, what I saw was worse!' a boy chipped in. 'It was like a huge white sheet being held out by four men. Straight and true in the wind like a flag.'

'Whatever form it takes,' Henry said firmly, 'it is up to no good and now one of our friends is dead as a result.'

There was nodding and mumbling from all.

So the people of Chester le Street got their hounds and traps. They lit torches and collected weapons. The whole angry crowd searched high and low. Some thought they saw a boy turn into a white eagle and fly away. Other said it was a white bat. But the shape-shifting creature was never seen again from that day on. The people of Chester le Street had driven it away but perhaps one day the brag will return to cause more mischief. So watch out, for who knows what form the brag will take next time.

11

THE PENSHER HILL FAIRIES

Penshaw Monument stands on Penshaw Hill. It overlooks Worm Hill, the place where the Lambton Worm wrapped itself around seven times to sleep. Penshaw Hill was once an Iron Age hill fort. But even before that, it was known as Pensher Hill. Now, many people visit the hill and monument for the phenomenal views but many years ago people would avoid it at all costs. This was because it was the home of fairies.

Owaine was riding past the hill. He had heard the stories but he had never seen any evidence of fairy folk anywhere near that place. Stories. They were just stories meant to scare little children and nothing more.

He grinned and galloped along. He was on his way to meet Isabel. He didn't have time to take the long route. He wanted as much time with that girl as he possibly could. Isabel lived on the other side of Pensher Hill. It would be madness to go any other way. The hill loomed large above him. Owaine did find himself looking up at it apprehensively. Suddenly, something was thrown right in front of him. His horse skidded to a halt.

Owaine looked down at the stone-strewn ground and saw a bucket. He furrowed his brow and jumped from the saddle. Where had it come from? He looked all about him. There was nobody around. The bucket was broken; two of the wooden slats were rotten.

'Fix that bucket,' a high-pitched squeak of a voice commanded.

Owaine looked around again. His eyes wildly scanned the landscape.

'Wh – Who's there?' he stammered.

'Fix that bucket,' the voice said again, this time more insistently.

'I might,' Owaine offered, 'but only if you show yourself.'

Just then, a sliver of light appeared on the hillside. It glowed yellow, then widened. It was a door. A rectangle of warm light was revealed right there on the hill. A very small creature then crawled out of the light. It was the size of a daffodil and wore green from head to toe. Its beady, doll-like eyes peered up at Owaine. It pointed at the bucket in the man's hands.

'Fix that bucket!' it shrieked.

Owaine smiled.

'What do I get if I do?'

'Butter,' came the shrill reply.

'Butter?' laughed Owaine. 'My Isabel makes the best butter in the county. Why would I want yours?'

'Fairy butter,' the creature squealed. 'It is like nothing you've ever tasted.'

Owaine rubbed his chin thoughtfully.

'All right,' he said at last. 'I'll bring it tomorrow.'

The creature nodded and walked back into the hill. The light was gone as the door slammed shut.

Owaine hooked the bucket onto his saddle and rode on. He would have quite a story to tell Isabel.

'You made a deal with the fairy folk?' she gasped, clearly horrified.

'Yeah!' grinned Owaine. 'So?'

'Don't you listen to stories?' Isabel asked.

'No!' snorted Owaine. 'They're for children!'

The pair argued back and forth for a while but then soon fell into one another's arms and the fairy in the hill was forgotten. The next day, Owaine returned home after galloping past the hill. He had fixed the bucket and decided to drop it off that evening on his way back to Isabel's. When he arrived at the hill, he stopped his horse at more or less the same spot as the night before.

'I have your bucket!' he called.

In the dim light of dusk the sliver of yellow light shone brightly upon the hill. The door was opened and the fairy stepped out.

'Have you fixed it?' the creature asked in high-pitched squeaks.

Owaine nodded and placed the bucket, which was bigger than the fairy, upon the path.

'Have you made my butter?'

The fairy nodded and dragged the bucket to the doorway. The creature squeezed the bucket inside and slammed the door firmly closed.

'Oi!' shouted Owaine. 'Where's my butter?'

Silence. Owaine's face reddened. He kicked at the grass ground of the hill where the door had closed.

'Give me my butter!'

The door was suddenly flung open.

'Be patient!' screeched the fairy. 'I was getting it!'

A large slice of rather delicious looking bread smothered in thick yellow butter was then offered to the man.

Owaine scooped it up and was about to take a large bite when something in the fairy's face made him stop. The creature wore an expression of cruel amusement.

'I'll have this later,' Owaine said quietly, 'Thank you.'

The fairy said nothing and watched the man with those empty black eyes. Owaine jumped back upon his horse's back and raced away. He flew to Isabel's to tell her the tale.

'You aren't really going to eat that, are you?' she asked.

Owaine was holding the bread and carefully peering at the butter.

'It smells delicious!' he sighed, breathing in the milky aroma. 'Yeah, I think I am.'

'Try it on your horse first,' Isabel suggested.

Owaine pondered this. Then nodded. He got up and went outside. Then he tore the bread in two and offered it to his stallion. The beast devoured it in one bite. It chewed noisily and Owaine smiled. He was about to bite into the other half when the horse's eyes widened. Its entire body stiffened. Then it slumped to the floor in a heap, clearly dead. Owaine hurled the bread that he was about to eat onto the floor. Isabel came racing out of the cottage at the sound of the falling horse.

'That fairy killed my stallion!' Owaine roared.

'Good job you didn't eat it then, eh?'

Owaine was furious. But Isabel managed to cool his temper and the pair fell fast asleep in one another's arms that night.

When the cockerel crowed the morning, Owaine got up sleepily.

'I'm going to have to walk home now, aren't I?'

Isabel stretched and yawned, nodding.

'I'll bury the horse tonight.'

He said his goodbyes and set off on foot, grumbling and griping the whole way. When he arrived at Pensher Hill, he stopped.

'You tricked me!' he shouted, kicking at the hill.

His feet slammed again and again into the sloping grass.

'Get out here and face me!' he thundered and roared. 'I'll teach you to trick me!'

Owaine shouted again and again. Then he stopped shouting. He didn't arrive at Isabel's that night. Nor the next. She went looking for him at his home but the neighbours said he never retuned home that day from the hill.

No one knows what happened to him. But every one knows it had something to do with the fairy in the hill.

12

THE GHOST OF HYLTON CASTLE

Roger Skelton had been missing for days. He had been working as a servant at Hylton Castle when he disappeared. Eventually he was found dead in the pond of the castle. It had been a murder. He had been killed with a scythe. His body was covered in straw to hide it for an entire day then it had been cast into the water when it was dark.

Robert Hylton had been arrested for the murder on 3 July 1609. It was claimed that he had ordered his horse to be sent for but it was not brought out as quickly as he had expected. Robert was then accused of killing the boy in the stable after finding him loitering there as opposed to doing his duties. But he was granted a pardon and found not guilty on 6 September of the same year.

Roger Skelton had been murdered but no one knew by whom. Suspicion was rife throughout the whole of Sunderland. It was all people talked about. But as the years passed, Roger Skelton was forgotten about.

Roger Skelton did not want to be forgotten about.

Roger Skelton came back.

When the maids slept in their beds, the boy could be heard making mischief around the castle. He would turn over the milk urns, smash plates in the kitchen, topple crates in the pantry, pull linen from drawers and knock chairs over in the dining room. He would pour water over the logs meant for the fire so that in the morning, when they were lit, the castle would fill with smoke. He would write his name on the kitchen floor in flour. He would place the saucepans next to the doors so that people would tumble over them the next day. Pewter tankards were left floating in the pond. Rugs would be rolled up. Bacon rashers would be put into shoes. Milk poured into boots. Apples would bob in the lavatory.

Not many maids lasted long at Hylton Castle. But then a new housekeeper was hired named Mary. She was kind and gentle. She had met ghosts before and knew how to handle them.

'Don't clean it up,' she told the maids. 'If he makes a mess again just leave it.'

The maids were surprised but did as they were told. That night, as before, there was clattering, banging and crashing. But in the morning everyone was surprised to see that the place had been cleaned. The noises in the night were Roger Skelton putting things right.

'It occurs to me that our ghost is mischievous because he is unhappy,' Mary told the maids, 'we need to give him jobs to do.' Well, the maids were delighted to hear that their workload was to be lightened. Even if it was at the hand of a ghost.

So, each day they would leave a room for Roger to clean and tidy. Sometimes the kitchen, sometimes a bedroom and sometimes the dining room. Occasionally the staircase or hallway or pantry. Now and again he even polished the silver. So time passed peacefully at the castle. Everyone was delighted with the new routine and being less busy.

But Mary still felt sorry for Roger. She wanted to meet him herself. So one night she sat herself in an armchair in a bedroom. The bedroom that the maids had left for Roger to tidy. She sat and she waited.

Moonlight spilled in through the window, casting dim white light over everything. At the stroke of midnight Mary felt a chill like she had never felt before. Twelve chimes rang out from the grandfather clock downstairs and on the last strike she shivered uncontrollably. Roger glided in through the closed door. He was a small boy, perhaps 8 or 9. He wore a coat of straw that seemed to be rotten and decomposing. His shoes were fashioned from bulrushes. He dripped freezing cold pond water. A clear shimmering mist of ice rose from his body as he busied himself in the bedroom, making the bed and sweeping the floor. His mournful expression made Mary feel sadder than she had ever felt in her life. She watched him work and shivered with the cold.

As the first light of dawn crept across the land, Roger then finished his work and glided back through the door leaving cold, wet footsteps on the floor. Mary called all of the staff into the dining room.

'That poor boy is cold,' she said to them. 'He needs some proper clothes.'

So the maids decided to make him shoes of the finest brown leather, a cloak of luxurious green velvet lined with white silk and a hat of beautiful red velvet. It was made by the tailor and presented to Mary before the day drew to a close. She laid out the fine clothes before a roaring fire in the kitchen.

That night Mary and the maids hid in the corner of the great kitchen to watch. They had left the place a mess so that Roger would know which room to go to. As the grandfather clock struck twelve times so the ghostly boy appeared, dripping and freezing cold. The spectators shivered but smiled when they saw the beaming boy look upon the outfit before the fire. He let the wet clothes fall to the floor and pulled on the cloak, hat and shoes. He seemed to lose some of his blue glow and instead seemed to radiate a warm orange, but that could have been the reflection from the fire.

Roger jumped in the air and clicked the heels of his new shoes together. Then he began to sing,

> Here's a cloak and here's a hood,
> The cold lad of Hylton will do no more good!

With that the boy disappeared. His ghostly form was never seen again. Some say that he went off to live with the fairies. Some say he rests in his grave. Others that he went to Heaven.

Mary and the maids missed the boy but the look of joy upon his face was something that they would never forget.

Wae's me, wae's me,
The acorn's not yet fallen from the tree,
That's to grow the wood,
That's to make the cradle,
That's to rock the bairn,
That's to grow to the man
That's to lay me!

13

The Dun Cow

'Tis certain, that the Dun cow's milk,
Clothes the prebend's wives all in silk;
But this indeed is plain to me,
The Dun cow herself is a shame to see.
from the Bishopprick Garland

The monks were exhausted. They had been travelling for days.
Their precious cargo had left Chester le Street and was headed
who knows where. Only God knew where. That was the problem
though. God knew but He hadn't told the monks. They wanted a
final resting place for their most prized and celebrated treasures.
They wanted a home for St Cuthbert. The Anglo Saxon monk had
been prolific in life, converting the people of Northumberland to
the Christian faith. But in death, he was equally busy!

His body had been buried on his home on the Holy Island of
Lindisfarne. It was sealed in a wooden coffin and buried under his
church. People came on long pilgrimages to visit the famous monk.
But when his coffin was moved many years after his death it was
discovered that he had not decomposed at all. The perfectly preserved corpse was the same as the day he had died. It was declared a
miracle and Bishop Cuthbert was renamed as St Cuthbert.

The monks of Lindisfarne told the many stories of his life
on their travels and more and more people wanted to pay their

respects to the man who was so blessed by God that he could talk to animals. He was still drawing people to the Christian faith even from a coffin. St Cuthbert's body was not the only treasure on this small island. There were the Lindisfarne Gospels too. But when Viking raiders arrived in AD 793, they too saw how wealthy and successful the monastery was. They stole valuable artefacts and took monks as slaves. They slaughtered and stole.

Fortunately some of the monks managed to escape the attack, and rescued not only the gospels, but also Cuthbert's body. They meant to travel to a monastery not dissimilar to their own. They headed for Ireland but a terrible storm was taken as a warning from God not to go there. So they roamed the land for years, eventually settling in Chester le Street. There, Cuthbert's body remained for over 100 years.

But now they were travelling again. The monks had been on the road for days. They wanted a sign. Any sign to say that they were taking the body of Cuthbert to the place he was meant to be. A final resting place worthy of such a man. Mostly, they carried him, three monks on each side of the coffin. But, when the terrain became too difficult to walk upon without risk of slipping and dropping the holy man, they used a wagon drawn by two horses. They were now upon such terrain. Their sandaled feet sank into soft, squelching mud. The horses whinnied and snorted with the effort and the strain of it.

'We're stuck!' cried a monk, pulling and tugging at the reins of one horse.

'We must continue,' gasped another, desperately pushing the hindquarters of their other horse.

Some monks heaved at the back of the wagon. But, the mud was a relentless monster. It devoured the wheels of the wagon as hungrily as it did the feet of the monks.

'Go back!' bellowed a monk. 'We must find another way!'

The others nodded in agreement. They tried to back up the wagon but it would not budge. The horses were becoming exhausted. The monks cried out in frustration. It was no good. The wagon was stuck in the mud nearly all the way up to the top of the wheels. The horses and the monks were stuck up to their knees.

'We must pray!' declared the monks.

And that is exactly what they did. They uttered prayers beneath their breath. They asked God for guidance. The prayers became silent. They waited for an answer.

The seconds seemed like hours. The panting of the horses and men lessened. Their breathing became less laboured and calmer. One monk snapped his eyes open.

'I know where to go!' he announced.

The other monks stared at him, their eyes wide and shining with anticipation.

'Did God speak to you, brother?' one monk prompted.

'What did He say?' gasped another.

'We are to take the body of our brother Cuthbert to Dunholme.'

The monks looked at one another.

'Where is that?' asked one.

The monk who had heard God was beaming with utter joy, but then his face fell.

'I don't know,' he finally said. 'I just heard in my head that we must take the body to Dunholme.'

The monks looked at one another once more.

Just then, a brown and white cow came walking past. It slowly, reverently even, padded on the soft grass nearby, heading towards a large patch of woodland. As it disappeared into the gloom of the trees, a girl came racing along.

'Have you seen my cow?' she asked, panting.

The monks nodded as one and pointed towards the woods.

'Oh thank goodness,' she gasped. 'I'm meant to be taking it to the market at Dunholme!'

With that, she raced off into the woods.

The horses suddenly moved forward. With a loud slurping they pulled free the wagon that held the body and began to follow the girl. The monks found that they were no longer stuck either. They moved effortlessly through the mud towards their precious cargo. They caught up to their horses and grabbed the reins. Cuthbert's body was lifted from the wagon. The monks carried him into the woods, following the girl and the cow. They stepped over the bracken and between the trees. On the other side they saw a hill surrounded by an oxbow of a river. It was a cloudy day but a burst of sunlight bathed the hill in a beam of golden light.

The monks smiled. The brown and white cow slowly walked down towards the place known as Dunholme and the monks followed. The body of Cuthbert was buried on the hill that overlooked the market. A church was built on top and the treasures had a new home.

Dunholme became a bustling, busy place but people began to call it by another name. It was known as Dunholme in Anglo Saxon times as Dun meant 'hill' and Holme meant 'island'. The place was renamed Dun Elm. In the time of the Normans it was called Duresme. They build a huge cathedral where the small church once stood.

That place is now known as Durham. It is the place where St Cuthbert still rests today and is the place where he still has thousands of people visit him every year.

> O'er northern mountain, marsh and moor,
> From sea to sea, from shore to shore,
> Seven years St Cuthbert's corpse they bore.
>
> He chose his lordly seat at last,
> Where his Cathedral huge and vast,
> Looks down upon the Wear.

from the Bishopprick Garland

14

THE EASINGTON HARE

The people of Castle Eden Dene had a problem. It was not a problem that they wanted to share with the other villages, for fear that they would be laughed at. Their problem was not a giant or a dragon or any form of terrible monster. No, their problem was a hare.

This furry creature would tease the greyhounds when they went coursing. It would dart in and out of the hedgerows and the dogs would follow. But the nimble hare would escape to the other side and the greyhounds would either become stuck, or wound themselves on vicious thorns.

Castle Eden Dene was famous for coursing. The people loved to hunt by sight rather than use bloodhounds to track scent. The rabbits round about were plentiful and it became great sport for the men to compete with one another as to whose hound could catch the most rabbits. People came from all over the county to watch the Saturday morning hunt.

But now this hare threatened to spoil it all. It would lure the dogs not only into hedgerow traps but also into the thick, tangled forest that grew next to Castle Eden Dene. The greyhounds would howl when they had lost sight of the hare and howl louder still when they could not find their way out of the spidery web of roots and bracken.

'I've had it with that hare,' fumed Paul. 'Listen to Merlin!'

His greyhound mournfully wailed from the forest ahead.

'Now I'm going to have to go in and get him,'

He stomped off, grumbling and cursing.

'We should hold a meeting,' Harry called after him, 'Decide what's to be done.'

More mumbling could be heard from Paul as he stepped into the labyrinth forest. Harry waited for his friend. He heard him before he saw him.

'Look at poor Merlin!'

Paul was carrying his dog in his arms. The sleek grey skin was covered in red scratches and deep scarlet gouges.

'That's it. Call a meeting!'

Harry nodded and set off. An hour later, everyone was gathered in the alehouse.

'Well,' Paul bellowed to quieten the crowd, 'what do we do?'

'Set traps!' John said. 'We could line the hedgerows. We could use your leeks, Harry.'

Harry shook his head.

'That hare is getting nowhere near my leeks.'

'We've tried traps,' Paul snapped, 'they don't work. We've tried shooting at the blasted thing but it's just too fast.'

'I don't think it's a hare at all,' Meg said while getting to her feet. 'It's not the right colour. It's black.'

'Of course it's a hare!' Paul shouted. 'What else could it be?'

'Hares aren't black.' Meg said flatly.

'It's a black hare. A new breed.'

Meg shook her head.

'It's not natural. It looks like a mole, only more agile.'

'Well if it's not natural,' Harry said, 'then we should go and ask Old Jim.'

This quieted the room for a moment. Old Jim knew things. If the horses got sick then it was Old Jim who knew how to heal them. If the water supply ran dry then Old Jim knew where the blockage would be. He knew why the hens wouldn't lay or why the milk from the cows was off. He just knew things.

Everyone nodded.

'Let's go now,' Paul said, 'before it's dark.'

They all filed out of the alehouse and set off out of the little village and up towards the other side of Castle Eden Dene.

Old Jim's cottage was set aside from the forest. It was an old, ramshackle thing. Tendrils of smoke were dancing out of the chimney and evaporating high above them.

'He's in,' said Paul, 'I'll knock.'

The crowd hushed as Paul's fist hammered the splintered wooden door three times. With a squeak like a rat being stretched, the door opened. Old Jim peered at his visitors.

'Afternoon Jim,' Paul began, 'you well?'

Old Jim didn't reply but merely regarded first Paul, then the rest of the crowd at his doorway.

'Trouble?' the old man croaked.

'I'm afraid so,' began Paul, and told the old man the whole tale of what had been happening with the hare. When he had finished, Meg stepped forward.

'It's not natural, I tell you.'

Everyone grumbled and she was shoved backwards.

'She's right,' grinned Old Jim toothlessly. 'It's not natural.'

All eyes were upon the old man for further explanation.

'Not natural things need catching with unnatural ways.'

The old man stepped out into the low afternoon sun. He pointed his pipe at a greyhound nearby.

'They're no good,' he said, 'you'll need a bloodhound from yonder.'

The pipe was now pointing in the direction of Hesleden.

'Once you've got the hound, it must be fed on human milk for three days and three nights. It's better to be a bloodhound as black as coal too.' With that, Old Jim went back inside his cottage and the door was firmly closed.

'I'll go and bake him a pie as a thank you.' said Meg.

'Harry and I will set off first light for the bloodhound.' Paul put in. Then they went back to the alehouse to discuss the matter further.

In the morning the pair went to Hesleden to borrow a bloodhound, preferably a black one, from the neighbouring village. The men were in luck and after a simple lunch returned to Easington with the black, slobbering dog.

'Now for the human milk,' sighed Paul.

'Jess has a newborn baby,' Harry said. 'If we ask her I'm sure she'll spare us some milk.'

After a lot of talking, persuading and eventually offering of money, the two men convinced the mother to spare a little milk for three days.

When the bloodhound was ready as per Old Jim's instructions, the whole village gathered together. The coursers began their usual hunt and, sure enough, the black hare arrived on schedule. Harry and Paul riled the bloodhound up and loosed it from its lead. The hare frolicked this way and that, seeming to enjoy having something new to taunt. But the bloodhound didn't race after the hare this way and that as the greyhounds did. It sniffed at the ground and followed. The dog lifted its muzzle to the air and snorted.

The hare darted and dashed in and out of the hedgerows and the bloodhound patiently waited for the hare's next move before padding along slowly after it. The hare seemed frustrated and zoomed into the forest. The bloodhound followed. Then the men followed too.

All day long the hare and the hound and the men circled this way and that through the forest. Finally, they arrived on the other side and saw the hare racing towards the village of Easington. It was then that the bloodhound made a mighty bound towards the hare. The dog moved at impossible speed and closed in on the black creature. The bloodhound sank its teeth into the hare's hind leg. A terrible screeching escaped from the hare's mouth. It frantically writhed and kicked with its free leg. Suddenly the hare broke free and hopped over the green then disappeared into the street beyond. The bloodhound sat and patiently waited for the men to catch up then, led the way. The tired men dutifully followed. The dog led them to a stone cottage on the other side of the green. It barked and howled mournfully at the door. Harry was first there. He hammered at the door with both fists.

'Open up!' he bellowed, 'Open up in there!'

The door swung open and the men pushed their way inside. They stared wide-eyed at what they saw.

There was no hare. But instead an old woman was sitting on the floor. She was holding her leg with both hands. Blood poured out between her fingers. She glared at the men above her.

'Look what your dog did!' she spat venomously.

The men backed out of the cottage.

'Witchcraft!' whispered Paul.

The dog was fetched and the men made a hasty retreat back into the forest and to their homes at the dene. Never again did they venture back to Easington. But neither did the hare ever return to Castle Eden Dene.

15

THE PICKLED PARSON

It was 1747 and Anna Garnage was in something of a pickle. Her husband was dead and she did not know what to do. She paced hurriedly over the graveyard of St Edmund's church in Sedgefield close to her home. John Garnage, her husband, was the reverend of the parish of St Edmund's and the pair lived in the rectory not far from the church. But now the body of her husband was sat slumped in an armchair in that rectory, very much dead, and Anna's mind was racing.

Her problem was that an annual tithe was to be collected from the parishioners of St Edmund's on 20 December. With her husband dead, the tithe would be null and void. It would still be collected, of course, but the money would go to the Bishop of Durham. He didn't need it! They did! They needed that money to live on for the year. It was their annual income. Well, *she* needed that money anyway. Without a husband, who would support her now? Anna circled the graveyard several times and still she had no plan. She had heard of clergymen who had died before the tithe could go to their families. She knew her fate. She would starve to death. She walked on. It was 10 December. Ten days before the tithe would be collected and delivered. What could she do?

She eventually walked back to her home with no decision made. After locking the front door, she walked into the living room and looked at her dead husband. He still looked so *alive*! If it were the twentieth now she would have no trouble at all convincing the parishioners that he was simply asleep. It was at this precise moment that a plan formed in her mind. Slowly, at first, like kindling igniting logs then eventually developing into a roaring fire. She now had her plan. She poured herself a brandy and sat opposite her husband.

'Oh John,' she sighed, 'I do hope you will understand. I do hope you won't mind.'

She sipped the brandy and felt it warm her inside. She needed her husband to be perfectly preserved for ten days. When the tithe was collected and delivered to her door she would sit her husband in the window and have him greet his loyal parishioners. Then, the next day, he would be found quite dead. She would be provided for over the following year while she played the grieving widow. After that, she would be free to find herself another suitable husband. Anna smiled. She knew that Tom the candlestick maker had always held a soft spot for her. He always looked at her that way. A year would be an acceptable length of time.

Once her brandy was finished, she checked the curtains were completely shut tight. She had to work quickly. She had to preserve poor dead John now.

Anna placed a bed sheet in front of the fire then moved her husband from the armchair and onto the sheet. She then removed his clothes. John usually wore a grumpy expression upon his face so she fashioned his calm, serene, even, death mask into a scowl. In order to delay rigor mortis setting in too soon she began rubbing the skin on his body from head to toe. It took a couple of hours but once his skin seemed fleshy and permeable she then went and fetched all of the brandy they owned from cabinets, cupboards and the larder. Anna then poured the lot into three buckets. She massaged brandy-soaked fingers all over his body.

Standing above the shimmering, glowing form of her dead husband, she suddenly had another idea.

Back in the kitchen, she found a large bag of salt. She then rubbed this all over John and gave a final coat of brandy.

It all took her several hours but at last he was fully dressed, embalmed and back in his chair facing the window. She had left herself just one glass of brandy from the three buckets but the smell of it made her feel sick so off she went to bed.

After only an hour or two's exhausted sleep, Anna opened the curtains to reveal her husband sitting in his chair with lifeless eyes looking out at Sedgefield going about its business.

So the days passed. Anna put it about the village that her husband was unwell and needed to rest for a week or so. Services were conducted by the deacon who was more than happy to have his moment of glory upon the pulpit.

There were well-wishers who came to the door but Anna simply told them that her husband was too unwell to get up from his chair. As they left Anna would crouch behind the chair and she would move John's elbow this way and that to give the people a cheerful wave.

When 20 December finally arrived, the deacon delivered the tithe to Anna. Two days later Reverend John Garnage had passed away peacefully in his chair looking out upon the village he loved so much. Well, that was what Anna had told everyone anyway.

'He hadn't been well for a couple of weeks,' Anna had said after the funeral, 'but I thought he'd recover.'

'This always seems to happen around Christmas,' the congregation added sadly.

Strange things began to happen once the funeral was over, though. Anna had many sleepless nights. There had been knocking and banging. Moans and groans. Shivers and chills.

There were all manner of ghostly sightings and apparitions. In the end, Anna did not spend her whole year grieving in Sedgefield, nor did she marry Tom the candlestick maker. She moved far away in fear and dread.

Another reverend was found. He and his family moved in. But again, they too complained of being haunted by the ghost of John Garnage in the rectory.

Eventually, in 1792, a lantern was knocked over and a fire burned the whole place down. Not a single sighting was ever recorded of John Garnage from that day on. Presumably the brandy-infused ghost went up in flames along with the building. Perhaps he now rests peacefully in Heaven ... a long way from his wife!

16

THE MONKEY HANGERS
OF HARTLEPOOL

During the Napoleonic War, Hartlepool was a small village in County Durham. It was a place filled with fear. Fear of an invasion from the French.

'They're everywhere, you know.' whispered William in the tavern.

'Who are?' asked John.

William hunched his shoulders and whispered for his companion to use a quieter voice, in hushed tones.

'The French,' he hissed, 'they're all around.'

'I've not seen anyone French,' laughed John. 'All I see are nets. And lobster pots.'

William shook his head.

'They're sneaky, you know. They can disguise themselves!'

'Don't talk nonsense. You wouldn't know a Frenchman if he bought you a pint!'

'Course I would, they're … well, they're …'

John laughed again and slammed two fists onto the table, making the glasses bounce a little.

'Go on then! They're what?'

'Ugly!' William replied at last. 'They're ugly and hairy!'

'That's the Scottish!' John guffawed. 'You're getting all mixed up.'

'Sure you're not from Scotland?' the landlord called out to them. 'You're both ugly and hairy.'

Suddenly the gloomy tavern was illuminated as the door was flung open.

'Warships!'

A dark silhouette stood in the rectangle of light. Silence occurred instantly. All eyes were upon the messenger.

'A whole fleet of warships! We can see them from the pier!'

The entire population of the tavern moved as one. They followed the messenger as fast as they could. A wave of words, all worried and frightened, accompanied the bustling crowd. More people stood and looked out across the water. It was true. Tiny, deadly looking vessels were on the horizon.

The sky seemed to sense the danger. The clouds turned from a light grey to great brooding beasts. They rolled over the heads of the onlookers.

'Look,' shouted William, pointing at the church behind them, 'God is making a storm to save us all!'

The onlookers nodded and agreed. Raindrops as big as apples fell from the sky. Thunderous clouds as black as canons sailed through the sky towards the Napoleonic fleet which was passing in the distance. Even from as far away as they were, the crowd could see the waves rise and fall. Lightening forked the sky. The priest from the church had joined them.

'God is saving our community,' he said as he arrived.

'Told you!' laughed William.

They were all drenched.

'We might as well go back to the tavern then,' suggested John.

Everyone looked at the priest.

'Well, it would seem there is little we can do here,' he said at last. 'Perhaps we should ride out the storm over an ale or two.'

A great cheer went up and the people of Hartlepool soon gathered in the tavern. Some stayed by the window and gave a steady report on the happenings in the distance.

'One of the fleet is in trouble!' Evelyn announced. 'It's moving away from the others! I think it's going to overturn!'

People pushed and shoved to get a better view of the sinking ship. It had indeed been knocked to its side. It was too difficult to see exactly what was happening.

'That's one down!' William laughed. 'Let's hope the others follow her down to Davy Jones's Locker!'

'God looks after His own!' the priest declared.

Everyone nodded. Eventually the storm passed and so did the rest of the fleet. But the party in the tavern did not. A full celebration went on for the rest of the night with more than just an ale or two being consumed by all. Finally, everyone went their separate ways and staggered home.

In the morning there was more commotion.

'There's wreckage!' a boy was shouting up and down the streets. 'There's wreckage washed up on the beach!'

People emerged from their houses and followed the boy. Sure enough, the sand was strewn with broken masts, ripped sails, snapped ropes and countless smashed pieces of wood of various sizes.

'Look what I've found!' screeched a delighted girl.

She held up a battered, dripping flag of red, white and blue vertical stripes. A huge cheer went up from all.

Suddenly the girl screamed and pointed to something that protruded from under a panel of sea-watered wood, stained white with salt. It was an arm. A small, hairy arm. Everyone gathered around in silence. The priest took a step forward nervously rubbing the wooden cross that hung around his neck. He kicked the wood away and people screamed.

A small body covered in thick black hair lay upon the ground. The figure wore a luxurious blue uniform decorated with golden buttons and tassels. A bicorn hat was stuck down firmly above a face with unusually large ears.

'Urgh!' gasped John, 'What is it?'

'I told you!' William declared triumphantly. 'People of Hartlepool … I give you … a Frenchman!'

People looked at him blinking uncertainly.

'Both ugly and hairy!' he went on.

Just then the hairy figure stirred and groaned.

'He's alive!' John pointed, with wide eyes.

Infectious fear spread like flames on tinder. Everyone turned and ran in multiple directions. They then hid behind the debris

of the ship that was strewn along the beach. The
uniform-wearing chimpanzee grunted as he sat
up. He scratched his weary head and staggered to his feet.

Williams took a step forward.

'Let's get him, lads!'

Worried looks were exchanged.

'It's a Frenchman,' William bellowed. 'Now do your duty for king and
country!'

There were nods and masks of determination were fitted firmly.
The crowd circled the ape as he finally got to his feet. He looked up to
see scores of hands reaching for him. Shrieking in alarm, the ape tried
to escape but was firmly held. They used the smashed ship's rigging to
tie him up then dragged him off along the beach.

'Wait!' bellowed the priest. 'We are God's people. There should
surely be a trial!'

Everyone stopped. There were nods all around.

'Very well,' agreed William, 'let's question him! Find out about
Napoleon's plans! We can send word to London. We'll be heroes!'

The ape was asked all about his ship, the passing fleet and what
the plans were for the war. To each of these he responded with
hysterical shrieking.

'Is that French?' asked John. 'I thought it was meant to be the
language of love.'

Upon getting no answers, the people of Hartlepool needed
another plan.

'We should hang the blighter!' William said triumphantly.
'Make an example of him!'

'We could use his own ship's mast as the gallows!' suggested Evelyn.
'Tie the tricolours of the flag to him too!'

That is exactly what they did. The unfortunate chimpanzee was hung
on the beach and to this day people from Hartlepool are known as
'Monkey Hangers'. The French ship's mascot is now the mascot for
Hartlepool United football club. His name is 'H'Angus the Monkey'.

17

THE FAERY IN THE QUARRY

John loved to listen to his grandmother's stories. Every Sunday, after church, she would sit by the fire and tell her tales. Dragons, giants, demons from hell. He adored them all. But it was the faery stories that he loved the most. Not the cute little fairies that helped princesses, but rather the mean, menacing faery folk like the one that lived in the quarry nearby. Now that was scary. It was a strong, powerful creature that could cause havoc if you crossed it.

John was sitting down, listening to a story that his grandmother told him came from Ireland about a boy who was taken by the faeries. A changeling had been left in the boy's place. This was a faery in disguise and the boy's father ended up throwing the imposter onto the fire. The boy was later rescued by his father from the faery hole. John gave his grandmother a huge hug before he set off home and thanked her for the story. His mind was full of this and all the other tales he had been told and he was not looking where he was going.

'Oof!'

The wind was knocked out of him as he landed on the floor. John looked up to see Edmund standing above him.

'Watch where you're going!' Edmund bellowed.

He was a huge boy, the same age as John, but twice the size.

'Sorry,' John said getting to his feet.

'You will be!'

Edmund shoved John back to the floor. Three other boys laughed at this. These were Edmund's acolytes who laughed at everything the burly boy did and said. The four boys then turned and walked away, still laughing.

'You're the ones who'll be sorry!' John called after them.

The four figures stopped abruptly. They turned at the same time to stare at John.

'What did you just say?'

Edmund was racing towards John in an instant. He turned to run away but the larger boy had slammed into him. Edmund wedged his knees onto John's arms and was sat upon his chest.

Raising a fist, Edmund leered into John's face.

'I'm going to beat you black and blue!'

'What are you boys doing now?' It was Tristan, the miller. 'Get off him at once!'

Edmund groaned and obeyed.

'You wait until I tell your father you've been up to your old tricks again!' Tristan said.

Edmund and his followers shrugged and walked off.

'I'll see you very soon, John!' he called over his shoulder.

'You all right?' asked Tristan.

John flushed scarlet and nodded.

'Stay away from those four,' the miller added and then walked away.

John walked slowly back to his home.

He was so tired of Edmund always at him. It was because he was smaller than all of the other boys. That was the only reason Edmund picked on him. John knew that he was seen as an easy target because of his height, but he also knew that he was braver than the lot of them put together. He would show them too. He would show them all.

A plan began to creep around the corners of his mind. He took his knife from his pocket and disappeared into the woods next to his village. There he made his way to a small cluster of rowan trees. He cut several pieces of bark from the tree and put them into his pocket. He then sheathed the knife and went back home. After supper he asked if he could borrow his father's horse.

'Just be back by dark,' his father had said. 'And watch out for adders!'

John smiled. It was a fine summer's night, which meant that it wouldn't be dark for ages. As for adders, the only snakes in the grass he would encounter were Edmund and his cronies.

John galloped off through one side of the village of Middridge and towards the other side. He saw the quarry in the distance and smiled. He felt a mixture of nervousness and excitement. He would show them. He would show them all. Edmund was busy tormenting a cat. He and his friends were squatted in a circle and took turns pulling the poor creature's tail and ears. It hissed and scratched at them and they laughed. As they were so engrossed in their torture, they did not notice John tying up his horse and strolling over.

'Still picking on things you think can't fight back?' asked John nonchalantly. 'You're so *brave*.'

The four stood up and the cat raced away.

'What do you want?' sneered Edmund. 'Want some more of this?'

The burly boy raised a meaty fist.

'I've come to dare you,' said John ignoring the threat.

Edmund was intrigued. His fist fell, his brow furrowed.

'Dare me to do what?'

'I dare you … to take my horse and ride to the quarry.'

'I'll take your horse and keep it!' laughed Edmund and the other three joined in.

'Then you have to ride around the quarry nine times and say the rhyme.'

Edmund stopped laughing.

'Don't be daft,' he said flatly. 'No one in their right mind would do that.'

'So you won't do it then?' John asked. 'Too scared?'

'You do it then,' Edmund said taking a step forward.

He jabbed a finger into John's chest.

'You ride up to the quarry.'

John smiled and nodded.

'All right, I will,' he said. 'You might be scared, but I'm not.'

With that, John turned and untied his horse. The four boys stood with mouths gaping open.

'He's not really going to do it,' Edmund scoffed. 'He's bluffing.'

'Let's follow him then,' one of the other boys suggested.

John grinned and trotted off towards the quarry. The four other boys followed on foot. John kept his pace slow to allow them to keep up, at a distance. When he arrived at the quarry, he peered into the entrance. It was a great, gaping black mouth. It seemed to be bottomless. An icy chill raced John's spine. The cold air that was breathed out of the hole gave him prickling goose bumps. The four boys arrived, panting breathlessly.

'You're not really going to do it, are you?' Edmund said at last.

'Watch me,' smiled John.

He trotted around the vast circle of darkness. When he had completed one circuit, he grinned at the other boys.

'Eight more to go!'

They looked at one another then back to the rider.

'You won't do it,' Edmund said, a little uncertainly.

After eight laps were completed, John stopped.

'This is the last one! I'd better say the rhyme. What is a gad anyway?'

'It's a wedge you drive into rocks with a hammer when you are trying to split them,' one of the boys answered.

'Oh, right,' smiled John, 'I've always wondered.' With that, he flicked his reins to complete the ninth lap of the quarry. As he neared the end of this lap he leaned over into the entrance and called, 'Oh faeries, oh faeries with your iron gads, You daren't come out and fight with Middridge lads!' John stopped. His voice echoed down into the quarry. Then there was silence. Suddenly a shrill and shrieking voice escaped the darkness. 'If your horse is not well hayed and corn fed, I'll have you before you get into bed!'

Edmund turned and ran, leaving the others.

'Get onto my horse!' shouted John.

The other three boys did not need telling twice. They clambered on top of one another. John kicked his heels to the horse and galloped off. As he raced past Edmund he grabbed the burly boy's jacket and heaved him up onto the saddle. The larger boy was slumped with his eyes firmly closed and crying out hysterically.

'Hurry up, John! Don't let the faery get us!'

With thunderous hooves, they galloped towards Middridge but all the while there was an ear-piercing screaming behind them.

John reached into his pocket and grabbed a piece of rowan tree bark. He dropped it and the shrieking momentarily stopped. But almost at once, it resumed and the chase was back on. John kept dropping more and more pieces of bark. He knew faery law. His grandmother had told him. A faery cannot pass a piece of the rowan tree without picking it up.

The five boys hurtled into the village and headed straight towards John's house. But the faery kept coming, wildly screaming and roaring with fury. They all jumped off the horse as it skidded to a halt outside the front door. John turned and hurled the last fistful of rowan bark and for the first time saw the faery. It was the size of a man and was covered in short green fur. Its long nose was curled in rage as it picked up the pieces of bark in its claw curved fingers. Shrieking again, it leaped forward.

John was the last one in and slammed the door closed. He kept his hands firmly against the wood but a heavy thud made him fall backwards. Then, nothing. No banging or shrieking. No blood curdling threats. John, shakily, stood up.

He turned and saw his parents and grandmother staring at him. His grandmother had her hands on her hips.

'Been to the quarry?' she asked angrily.

'Maybe,' sighed John.

He smiled at her then walked to the door. He opened it just a fraction.

'No! Don't!' cried Edmund, with tear-streaked cheeks and wild eyes.

John ignored him and peered through the crack.

'Its all right,' he said, 'it's gone.'

When John opened the door wide, a spear was stuck on the outside. It was buried deep inside the wood.

'That was close,' the boy said, turning to look at the others.

'Wow,' said one boy, 'you saved us!'

'Yeah,' said another, 'thanks John.'

'How did you know about the pieces of bark?' asked the third. John smiled. He took his grandmother's hand.

'I listen to stories,' he said simply.

'Get that horse in the stable,' his father said. John nodded.

'I'll make your new friends some supper,' his mother said.

'Come on lads,' Edmund said, wiping his cheeks. 'Let's go and help John.'

So they did.

Oh faeries, oh faeries with your iron gads,
You daren't come out and fight with Middridge lads!

If your horse is not well hayed and corn fed,
I'll have you before you get into bed!

18

THE SOLDIER IN THE WALL

A small hill overlooks the north bank of the River Wear. From this hill the cathedral dominates the spectacular view. On this hill stands Crook Hall. It is Durham's hidden secret. The house was built in 1286 and is one of the oldest homes in the city. It nestles within a cluster of six acres of secret gardens. The house and hall is a mixture of medieval, Jacobean and Georgian designs.

But it is the hall itself that hold a dark secret. A secret that is within the very walls themselves.

The hall is guarded by pear trees to ward off evil spirits, and the door bears carved symbols to keep witches away. There are three circles etched into the wood. They are joined together and sit above other circular designs. Rowan tree branches used to be hung above them to enhance the power of protection.

However, it is what happened on the inside rather than the outside of this hall that makes mediums and ghost hunters run in terror even to this day.

The medieval hall had been decorated for a dinner party. The servants were bustling in and out of the hall carrying platters of food. They scurried with heads bowed low, to and from the kitchen, onto the screens passageway and finally entering the hall then back again. The family who lived there at the time had invited many important guests from the city and everything had to be perfect.

Cold food was sitting on long tables in the hall and the hot food was being kept warm in the kitchen. Everything was ready.

It was at this point that the bell was rung. The sound danced down the passageway and the servants scattered to unseen places. Cuthbert Billingham nodded approvingly. One servant answered the ringing bell and flung the door open.

'Welcome to Crook Hall, sir,' the servant said, gesturing for the guest to enter.

A soldier strode inside, nodding curtly at the servant.

'Ah, you're back then,' Cuthbert said gruffly. 'You look well.'

Jack nodded.

'Crook Hall,' he said, 'where's that name from? The river perhaps?'

Cuthbert shook his head.

'Lots of people think that, but no. Its original owner was Peter Del Croke. Croke became Crook.'

'Ah, I see,' Jack smiled.

'Drink?'

The soldier nodded.

A servant emerged from a wall bearing a pewter tankard. Jack snatched it up and the servant seemed to camouflage himself back into the wall.

'Who else is coming?' asked Jack.

Before Cuthbert could reply, the bell both interrupted and answered the soldier's question. The servant ushered the rest of the guests inside the hall. There were several couples, all smiling and bowing as they entered.

Cuthbert made the introductions, most of which were unnecessary but Jack heard none of this. He was utterly hypnotised by the woman who entered the hall first. She had raven hair and scarlet lips with skin of alabaster. She was reminiscent of a fairy-tale character. Jack strode over, took her hand and kissed it. His lips lingered a fraction of a second too long. Servants interrupted the awkward moment by arriving with the warm food.

'Come!' bellowed Cuthbert. 'It is a cold night and we should warm ourselves with food and drink.'

Throughout the feast, Jack could not take his eyes off the lady. This had not gone unnoticed by the other guests, including her own husband. His cheeks had reddened increasingly throughout the meal. His temper darkening at this blatant disrespect being so publically displayed.

Jack ignored all questions from the other guests and spoke only to this mysterious lady who he had not met before. She smiled coyly at all of this attention and replied succinctly and politely. She turned herself towards her husband but Jack would not be deterred.

'Perhaps after dining, we could take a stroll through the gardens?' Jack said, all teeth. 'Get to know one another a little better without all of this noise. Without all these distractions.'

He had meant this as a whisper but the hall had fallen silent as he said the words. All eyes were upon him.

The lady's husband stood up. Now all eyes were upon him.

'What the devil do you think you're doing?' bellowed the husband. 'That's my wife! The impertinence of it!'

Jack was up in an instant. His expression a mask of defiance. He kicked away the heavy wooden chair.

The silence in the room was tangible. Jack took two steps towards the man. He grinned sarcastically.

'What do —'

The soldier said no more. He was suddenly silenced. His eyes widened. They rolled down his body. There was a knife sticking out of his belly; the husband was still holding it. A red circle was growing through Jack's his clothes.

The man stepped backward, letting go of the knife. Jack lurched backwards a step and pulled free the knife. It clattered to the stone floor. He gasped and held his wound.

'Somebody —'

Jack did not finish these words either. He staggered backwards then fell to the floor. Everyone looked at Cuthbert. He was standing now and looked first at Jack and then at the husband. Back and forth his gaze went.

'Somebody help me!' screamed Jack.

He was slumped against the wall. Next to him was a doorway that held a large standing candle. It had been empty when the hall was first designed and was never actually used as a door. The candlelight flickered inside casting gloomy shadows. Cuthbert stepped towards Jack. The soldier held his belly with one hand and stretched out the other to grab the host. Cuthbert roughly pulled Jack to his feet. Then pushed him into the empty doorway. He fell and sent the candle falling too.

'What are you doing?' asked a guest.

'He'll die!' another said. 'Fetch a servant!'

Cuthbert whirled around to face his guests.

'Crook Hall does not need the scandal,' he barked. 'I've had enough trouble with this water supply business. I don't need a scandal.'

Jack was trying to get to his feet. He was grunting with the effort as blood spilled onto the floor.

'You have nothing to fear, my lord,' Cuthbert said to the husband, whose mouth was opening and closing in astonishment and horror. Cuthbert placed a hand on his shoulder. 'I'll take care of this,' he said soothingly. The guests all looked at one another. 'I think it's time we bade each other a good evening,' Cuthbert continued. 'And not a word to anyone. Are we clear?'

There were nods as people exchanged worried glances. The first to leave was Jack's attacker and the object of his desire. The other guests soon followed. Jack was deathly white now and slumped in the shadows. Cuthbert had called for his most trusted servants.

'Seal him in.'

The servants looked at their master.

'Brick it up.'

After a few moments hesitation, they obeyed.

Despite his exhaustion from the massive blood loss, Jack screamed throughout the whole entombing. As the last brick made the darkness complete he began to moan and sob. Cuthbert could hear it even through the newly made wall. He stood there and listened until there was silence.

When the last of the plates were cleared away and the candles had been snuffed, Cuthbert went to bed.

Years passed.

The hall was passed on from the Billinghams to the Mickletons then onto the Hoppers and in 1793 it was passed on to Reverend Hopper Williamson who leased it to Canon James Raine. He was a friend of William Wordsworth who was a regular visitor to the hall and gardens.

The hall itself had been used for hosting great feasts and parties throughout this time, all under the shadow of the sealed doorway. James Raine was hosting a party one night and the guests were gathered in the screens passage. He wanted to surprise them. He had a lavish feast prepared. A feast not dissimilar to the night that Jack was murdered. The tables were heaving under the weight of the steaming hot dishes. James was dramatically holding the heavy tapestry that divided the hall from the passageway. He wanted to unveil the hall when all were gathered and ready.

Suddenly an immense and thunderous banging was heard from the hall. James pulled up the tapestry to see utter devastation. The tables were turned and the food was scattered everywhere. The bewildered guests looked at James Raine. The canon was utterly baffled.

'There was no one in here,' he gasped. 'Who could have done this?'

Years passed again.

The hall was passed on to the Fowlers then to the Hawgoods. Over the fifteen years that the Hawgoods lived in the property, Mary Hawgood reported that knives from the kitchen were constantly disappearing. The sort of knives that were used to kill Jack the soldier.

Crook Hall now belongs to Keith and Maggie Bell who host weddings in the house, grounds and the medieval hall. Recently, a caterer was setting up a table in the hall, next to the sealed-up doorway. She was setting the places for the guests. As she put the knife down she felt a hand of ice push her. She fell onto the table, sending cutlery clattering. She ran in terror from the hall and told the owners what had happened.

Jack still sits behind that doorway. Jack doesn't like feasts in the hall. Jack wants to be left alone.

19

THE SCULPTOR ON THE MARKET SQUARE

Charles William Vane Tempest Stewart was the Marquis of Londonderry and an important man in Durham. He owned many of the coalmines surrounding the city and used a lot of his personal wealth to make sure they ran better and had safer conditions for the men who worked down the pits. He commissioned the building of Seaham harbour so that the coal could be transported to any location. As well as being a prominent businessman who brought a huge amount of trade to the region, he was also a soldier who had fought in many battles. The statue of Lord Londonderry in Durham's market square shows him atop a horse wearing his Hussar's military uniform. It stands in the very centre of Durham city surrounded by the cathedral, castle and river. It takes pride of place.

Raffaelle Monti, a Milanese artist, was commissioned to create a double life-sized figure of the man on his horse. It was unveiled on 2 December 1861 to an admiring crowd.

'I give you … my perfect statue!' Monti had boasted to the onlookers.

There was rapturous applause. It was the perfect addition to the bustling square. A fitting tribute to the man who invested his money and time to make the county a better place.

Monti was taken to the tavern on the market place and bought drink after drink. He was praised for his work by many and in the celebratory atmosphere, the sculptor made a claim that became the talk of the city.

'If anyone,' Monti had slurred, 'anyone, can find a mistake on my perfect sculpture, then I will join Lord Londonderry in the afterlife. I will kill myself!'

People laughed, but people talked. The story spread far from the city and right across the county. Anyone who visited the market square was challenged to find error in the sculpture but no one could. Travellers from across the world pondered the statue. They inspected it closely but not one mistake could be found. The statue was indeed perfect. Or so it was thought for many years.

On one particular day, many years later, a blind beggar arrived in the city. The kind people of Durham gave him what they could spare, food and a little to drink. But they also described to him their amazing home with pride. The glorious cathedral and beautiful castle was discussed at length. As too was the statue of Lord Londonderry and Monti's boastful claim.

'I'd love to see it all,' the beggar had said, 'but alas my sight left me many years ago.'

The people nodded and sympathised.

'I use my hands to see now,' laughed the beggar, 'I feel things and create a picture of them inside my own head for me to see alone.'

'Well, we'll help you up onto the plinth of the statue then,' one person suggested. 'Let you have a feel of it!'

There was nodding of heads and clapping of hands. The people of Durham thought this a most excellent idea. So the blind beggar was taken to the plinth and he was raised upward. The man steadied himself on the sandstone pedestal and began to feel the bronze horse and rider.

Soon a crowd gathered beneath the base and looked on. The beggar was continually asked if he had found any mistakes in the work but he said nothing and continued to rub the bronze beneath his fingers.

Word of the blind beggar's tactile assessment reached the ears of the sculptor Monti himself. He made his way down to the market square to see the crowds beneath his masterpiece.

'Here comes Monti!' one of the crowd announced. 'There's no word from the beggar yet mind!'

The sculptor was silent and as still as his creation. He wordlessly watched the blind beggar as he shuffled around the plinth, smoothing his hands over man and beast.

The sun slipped slowly to the west. The shadows of the three characters atop the pedestal grew longer. More people gathered to watch.

Eventually, the beggar stopped. He turned and faced the hushed crowd.

'Can someone help me down please?' he asked.

'Certainly not!' spat Monti. 'Not until you can tell us what you have felt! Say it, man! The statue is perfect!'

All eyes were upon the beggar. Only a few seconds passed but it seemed a lifetime.

'It is indeed a fine piece of work,' the beggar began.

Monti's expression was incredulous. His cheeks reddened and his eyes darkened.

'It is indeed, *almost* perfect.'

The sculptor opened and closed his mouth several times but no words emerged. He looked like a fish taken from the Wear gasping for air.

'Yes indeed,' the beggar said again. 'Almost perfect.'

Finally, Monti found his voice.

'Almost perfect?!' he spat. 'What on earth do you mean?'

The crowd looked from the sculptor to the beggar. They too wanted an explanation almost as much as Monti himself.

'Well, the rider is flawless but the horse is not.'

Everyone began to scan the horse for any flaws.

'What's wrong with it?' demanded Monti.

'It is perfect in every way. Except, the horse has no tongue.'

The crowd rushed to peer into the mouth of the horse.

'He's right!' declared one.

'There's no tongue!' gasped another.

'It's not perfect!' laughed a third.

The beggar was helped down and all turned to look at Monti. But he had gone. He fled the market square and was never seen again in Durham.

Some thought he had gone through with his promise to end his own life. Many told tales of his dramatic suicide right there on the market square that very night. But he had actually returned to Milan after living in England for less than a year. The statue still stands in Durham today and some think the horse does have a tongue while others disagree. To be certain you need to see it for yourself.

20

LILY FROM LUMLEY

Sir Ralph Lumley had done well. He had commanded his troops in Berwick masterfully, and successfully drove the Scots back northward in 1388. He and his men had held the wall and he was in royal favour.

After this success, it was in that same year that he had been asked to lead the attack against the Scots again, at the Battle of Otterburn. The border skirmishes had been happening more and more frequently and Sir Ralph was told, in no uncertain terms, that failure was not an option.

But the English were defeated. Some say it was the rashness and boldness of Harry Hotspur that was to blame. But whoever was to blame did not matter to Sir Ralph. He had been captured and imprisoned by the Scots. He was taken over the border into Scotland. There he remained in thick coils of heavy chains to contemplate his woe. It had been such a decisive victory for the Scottish that Sir Ralph knew it would be some time before the two armies met again.

It was a long, hard year. But eventually, once payment had been made, Sir Ralph was released and returned to his home. This mighty manor house had been built by his ancestors and was a welcome sight for the weary knight. He had been given a lot of time to think while in his dreary dungeon. One thought that kept coming back to him, the thought that had kept him going during long days and even longer nights, was the idea to convert his home into a castle worthy of a knight. The castle would serve as a reminder of his victories in battle rather than this failure. The castle would stand atop a hill overlooking Chester le Street and beyond.

Sir Ralph wasted no time in petitioning the Bishop of Durham for permission to start the building works as soon as possible. This he did and in the same year of his release from prison, 1389, stonemasons and builders had set to work.

Sir Ralph's son, Thomas, and his wife, Lily, would have the home of their dreams. Sir Ralph himself would have the castle as a symbol for his greatness. His legacy would live on. But there was a problem. Richard II was to be deposed in 1399 and replaced by Henry IV from the House of Lancaster. Richard had exiled Henry before he could claim the throne. Henry fled to France and plotted his return. Everyone knew of Sir Ralph's support for Richard II. If Henry did indeed successfully return to England, it would spell trouble for Sir Ralph. So the knight and his son travelled south to London to find what news they could. While they were away, the rumours were rife around Chester le Street. The castle on the hill was the home of traitor. Lily had not been to church for months. No one had seen her. She had become a virtual recluse. The people were restless.

Two priests were sent to the castle to confront Lily about her apparent lack of faith. Why was she not attending church? Why had she not left her castle for so long? The priests were met with cold hostility from Lily.

'Who are you to question my faith?' she screamed at them. 'On whose authority do you dare to speak to me like this?'

The enraged priests grabbed Lily.

'We represent God's authority on earth!' they bellowed. 'Who are *you* to question *us*?'

There was a scuffle. Lily bit and scratched at them in her fury.

'She is possessed by the devil!' one priest declared.

'We must exorcise her!' the other shouted.

The pair fought the hysterical lady and eventually Lily was pushed into the castle well, where she fell to her death.

The priests looked fearfully around them. No one had seen the murder. No one would know.

They whispered in hushed tones to one another about what they could do. Together they came up with a devious plan.

The priests travelled to a nearby village. There they found a sick woman on her deathbed. They asked the family if they could take care of her. They told them that they would take her to a nunnery and make her a sister of God. She would be well looked after and when she died she would be seated at God's side in eternal bliss.

The priests further persuaded her with talks of infection and the spread of disease to the rest of the family. The family eventually agreed and the priests took the poor woman to the local nuns. She was indeed cared for, but died after only a few days.

The priests told Sir Ralph and his son, Thomas, that Lily had decided to become a nun in their absence. They convinced the father and son that she had become sick and died in the nunnery. Sir Ralph and Thomas believed the whole tale and attended the funeral of the sick woman thinking that it was Lily.

Not long after this, Henry IV was crowned king after being accepted as the rightful monarch by parliament. Sir Ralph and Thomas were both arrested and stripped of their titles. Father and son were imprisoned and eventually beheaded in 1400.

The castle was given to the Earl of Somerset. As the Earl had no son, it was then passed on to Sir Ralph's grandson, Thomas Lumley. Sir Thomas Lumley became a heroic and successful solider. He played a major part in the War of the Roses, led the siege of Bamburgh Castle and fought side by side with Edward IV against the Lincolnshire Rebellion.

Sir Thomas's son, George, succeeded him and the castle finally became a hotel in 1976.

Throughout its occupancy, though, there have been sightings of a ghostly figure, dripping wet and rising from the well. Lily of Lumley. Lily haunts Lumley Castle to this day. Her restless spirit has been seen countless times and if you visit you might just see her for yourself.

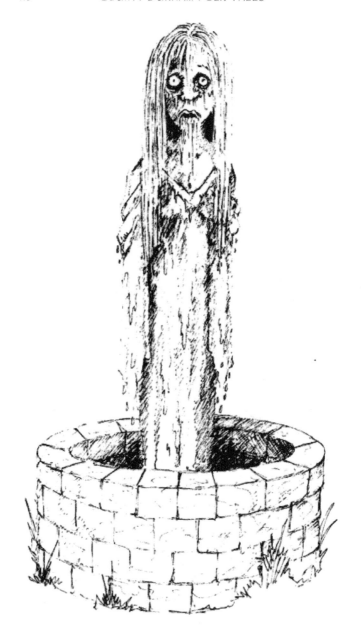

21

THE STANHOPE FAIRIES

There was once a girl called Bessie who loved to walk her dog by the Wear. The dog was a spaniel and never left the girl's side. On one unusually bright and sunny day she heard a sound unlike anything she had ever heard before. It was a tinkling, ringing sound that was coming from a little cave on the riverbank.

'What's that, Charlie?' she asked her spaniel.

The dog raced over to the cave, splashing through the river. The sound stopped. Bessie carefully stepped over the smooth stones to the other side and peered in herself. Inside the cave she saw a group of tiny people. Each one held a musical instrument made of wood or brass. They were fairies.

'Charlie, come on!' Bessie scooped up her dog and ran.

She knew better than to cross the fairy folk. She knew they were dangerous. She hoped that they wouldn't be too upset that she had interrupted their music.

When she got home she told her father all that had happened.

'This isn't good,' her father sighed. 'We need to go and see Aubrie. She'll know what to do.'

The girl and her father walked to the market square, then continued beyond towards the river accompanied by Charlie. As they passed Castle Heugh they saw a small thatched cottage.

Bessie's father knocked at the door. The smell of an open fire mixed with strong herbs filled their nostrils as the door opened.

'Ah, Finton,' Aubrie rasped, 'nice of you to visit. With little Bessie too! Not so little now though, I see. Come in.'

The pair entered the cottage and saw all manner of peculiar things on shelves, tables and benches. There were bones and feathers, jars and bottles, books and parchments, all strewn about in no particular order.

'Bessie saw fairies,' Finton began, 'down by the river. She interrupted their music.'

Bessie looked down at the floor. She rubbed Charlie's ears.

'That is not good,' sighed the old woman. 'But there's hope for you yet.'

Father, daughter and dog looked at the old woman with wide eyes.

'The fairies will come for Bessie tonight,' Aubrie continued wearing a wrinkled, serious expression upon her face. 'They will take her away.'

Finton gasped.

'Unless no sound comes from your home. No sounds from man nor beast. No sound from anything.'

Finton nodded quickly.

'We can do that. Thank you Aubrie.'

'Stay for a cup of my special tea. I haven't seen you for an age!'

Finton laughed and relaxed in the company of his old friend.

When they returned home, Finton cooped up all of the hens so they would sleep quietly. Then he latched the gate so that it would not rattle in the wind. Next he stopped all of the clocks in the house so that they would not tick. He put out the fires in case they crackled and spat. Locking the door, he called for his daughter.

'Straight to bed, Bessie,' he said, 'and remember, not a sound tonight.'

She nodded and hugged her father. She lay under the covers but was wide awake in case she snored. Her father sat in his chair and moved not a muscle.

The minutes turned to hours and still the pair remained awake. Then, in the darkness and the silence, a sound emerged. It was the same tinkling, ringing sound that Bessie had heard down by the river.

The fairy musicians had come for the girl but soon stopped. It was silent and they could not enter the house unless a sound was heard. It was fairy law and that was that.

Just then the sleeping spaniel awoke. He heard the music from earlier. He sensed his owner was in danger and let out a loud yap.

The fairies flew up to Bessie's window. They lifted it and flew inside. They pulled free the covers and pulled the girl from her bed. Charlie barked and barked. Finton raced upstairs but as he entered his daughter's bedroom, she was already gone.

'No!' he screamed. 'No! No! No!'

The dog was racing in circles, barking nonstop. Finton scooped up the distraught dog.

'It's not your fault, it's mine!' he said through his tears. 'I should have fed you so much that you slept. I should have made you sleep next door. I should have thought you'd try and protect her!'

Finton then put Charlie beside the bed and raced down the stairs. He was racing to the river and towards Aubrie's house. He slammed his body against the wood and pounded at the door. Aubrie opened it and Finton fell inside.

'Help me!' he gasped. 'Oh please help me!'

'The fairies took her?' the old woman asked.

Finton nodded through his tears.

'I can help you still!'

'How?'

The old woman spoke in soothing tones.

'Go to the cave of the fairies. Take with you a branch from the rowan tree, that will protect you.'

Finton nodded.

'But to win your daughter back you will need three things. You need to take a light that does not burn, a chicken with no bones in its body and an animal that will give you part of its body without losing a drop of blood. If you do this then fairy law says that your daughter must be returned to you.'

Finton slumped back into his chair. He was dumbfounded. How would he find the three impossible things?

'But you must be quick! If you do not claim your daughter before dawn then she will be lost to you forever!'

He nodded and jumped to his feet. He thanked Aubrie and ran from the cottage. As he crossed the Castle Heugh he almost stumbled on a beggar who was sleeping at the side of the market square.

'I'm sorry,' Finton said. 'Here, take this.'

He threw a coin for the old beggar. The man caught it and said,

'You are kind and I can help.'

Finton wore a befuddled expression and saw the man reach towards him, his hand cupped.

'A glow worm makes light that does not burn.'

The beggar dropped the little worm into Finton's hand.

'Thank you!' he gasped.

Placing the worm, carefully in his pocket he ran for home.

A barn owl swooped down before him and caught a mouse. Finton ran past and clapped his hands. The owl dropped the mouse and flew away. The mouse scurried to Finton's feet.

'Thank you!' the mouse squeaked. 'You saved my life! There is an egg in your hen house buried under straw. It has been there for fifteen days unnoticed. It holds a baby chicken that has not yet grown any bones!' With that, the mouse scampered off.

Finton smiled.

He ran again and heard a high-pitched crying from a hedge. He raced over and saw a rabbit caught in a trap. It writhed and moaned. So Finton freed it from the snare.

'Thank you!' peeped the rabbit. 'I would have been in a stew by morning! If you grab a lizard by its tail then it will escape by leaving the tail in your hand without losing even one drop of blood. There are lots of them down by the river near the fairy cave.' The rabbit then hopped into the hedgerow and disappeared.

Finton beamed.

He sprinted to his house and collected a rowan branch from the tree in the garden. Then he found the egg in the hen house and rushed to the river. There he saw lizards sleeping under the smooth stones. He grabbed one by the tail. It dragged itself away, leaving the tail in Finton's hand.

His eyes scanned the river. He remembered Bessie's description of the fairy cave. Even in the darkness he could see the opening. It was darker than everything else. A small, gaping mouth that had devoured his daughter.

He peered inside. Nothing.

Then, a tinkling, ringing sound escaped the mouth of the cave. Finton got the glowworm and held it to the darkness before him. It lit the small space and he saw the fairies inside. He rolled the egg towards them and pushed in the lizard tail.

The music stopped.

Bessie hands suddenly appeared. Finton grabbed them and pulled his daughter up and out of the fairy home.

Hand in hand they ran back to their home and neither of them ever returned anywhere near to the fairy cave of Stanhope.

22

THE GREY LADY OF DURHAM CASTLE

The Castle of Durham is majestic and magnificent. It stands proudly beside the cathedral as the perfect partner. The inside holds an ancient chapel. The pillars of this are decorated with numerous beasts and even a mermaid. Christianity and paganism blend together in the form of Jesus as a Green Man figure upon the walls. It was a device used by the early church to lure the pagans inside and convert them to the faith.

Isabella Van Mildert lived in the castle in the nineteenth century. She was content and happy there. She loved to walk to the market square and immerse herself in the hustling, bustling city. The traders shouted and bartered with one another. The smells and tastes in the air were rich and varied.

Her family would often tell her off for spending so much time out of the castle. They would complain that she should be spending more time embroidering and reading, not frolicking with the folk in the city. But she didn't care. She did enjoy living in the beautiful castle, but she was lonely. She longed to be with others of her own age.

One winter's night, she sneaked out of the castle and down towards the market square. She wanted to see it at night. She knew the taverns would be busy and she had no intention of going inside but rather she simply wanted to see Durham at night for herself. Isabella pulled a large cloak around herself and lifted the hood over her head. The heavy, grey material would disguise her. She smiled from beneath the cloak.

As she passed the Palace Green she stopped and looked at the cathedral and castle illuminated in the moonlight. The two buildings seemed to glow. Isabella then scurried along, holding the cloak tightly around her body. She headed down towards Saddler Street, which would lead her to the square.

The Shakespeare pub window glowed with dim orange light. Laughter boomed from within.

She stood and peered through the small, smudged windows. It was then that Isabella heard the clopping of hooves upon cobblestones. She turned and saw a dark figure riding a black horse up the lane. This figure was cloaked and hooded like she was.

She watched him pass by, but then he stopped. He turned his head towards her.

Goosebumps immediately spread over her entire body as the rider turned the horse and stepped forward. He loomed above her, immense and intimidating. She bit her lip and was unsure whether or not to speak.

The dark rider opened his cloak to reveal gleaming white ribs. His hood fell unveiling a skeleton face. The lifeless, empty eyes bore down upon her.

Isabella's locked legs imprisoned her body. She could not move. It was as if this skeletal figure had turned her into a statue. The rider placed the hood back upon his head and turned the horse to walk away.

She remained there a few moments more until the door of the Shakespeare was flung open exposing her to a cacophony of noise. This spurred her into action. She ran back to the castle. It was only as she burst inside that she realised that the dark rider had travelled in the same direction. He could be in the courtyard now.

The terrified girl ran up to her bedroom. She raced up the black staircase. But, in the dim light offered by the moon, the girl stumbled and tripped. Her cloak was trapped under her feet and she fell backwards. She tumbled down, down, down.

With a terrible cracking sound, her head slammed against the stairs. Her neck was broken and her lifeless body plummeted down the last few stairs then slumped at the bottom under the grey cloak.

Years passed.

The castle became the home of university students. One of the first students was Frederick Copeman in the early nineteenth century.

He had worked hard to be accepted at the university. His family was so proud of him.

Frederick spent a sleepless night in his room. He lived above the Black Staircase where Isabella had died. His room was number twenty-one.

Frederick was anxious as the results of his degree were to be posted on the notice board on Palace Green the next day.

He was first in line the following morning. The notice board had been organised so that those who had received first-class degrees were listed on the piece of paper at the top of the board. Those with second-class were on the piece of paper pinned to the middle. Those with third-class degrees were on the paper at the bottom. If you had failed to pass the degree course then your name was not on any of the three papers.

Frederick scanned the pages in front of him.

He was not there.

He read the names again and again and again. Eventually, he was pushed out of the way by the other students who were desperate to see how they had done themselves.

Frederick was devastated. He tore back up to his room. There, he could be heard pacing and sobbing. He languished in his sorrow all that day.

His fellow students knocked upon his door but he had it firmly locked and ignored them all. That night, while the others all went out to celebrate, Frederick mourned. He had tried his very best and he had failed. He had let his family down.

Once certain that the castle was empty, he slowly and sombrely descended the staircase towards the Palace Green. Hope had crept into the corners of his mind and he had decided to check the notice board one last time.

But as he descended the Black Staircase he saw someone at the bottom of the stairs. A grey-cloaked figure stood motionless. The hood covered the features.

'Who – Who's there?' asked Frederick uncertainly.

The figure looked up revealing a pale girl with a gaunt face.

'I'm lonely, Frederick,' she said.

Her voice carried its own echo. She hadn't moved her lips.

'I'm lonely,' she said again.

Frederick stood hesitantly upon the stairs.

'We can be together,' the ghostly voice resonated up the stairs. 'We can be together forever.'

Frederick shook his head. He was imagining this. It was caused by the stress of the day.

He closed his eyes tightly. When he opened them, she was gone. He shook his head again and walked down the stairs.

Frederick then ran to the noticeboard. He scanned the three pages as they flapped in the wind.

His name was not on there. He wailed in woe. He sank to his knees and sobbed. Then he decided to pay a visit to the cathedral. He would find solace there. He would find peace.

The sanctuary knocker rapped on the wooden door as he opened it. The cathedral was unlocked and deserted. He walked up the aisle towards the tower. He climbed the spiral stairs to the top.

There he looked out first at the castle then across the city.

What would his family think? What would they say?

He then heard footsteps upon the stairs.

Who could it be? He just wanted to be alone. Why could he just not be left alone?

The grey hooded figure from the castle was there once more. Her hood fell. She had raven black hair that seemed to move by itself. It was like she was underwater. Her translucent skin shone a white pale blue.

'I'm lonely Frederick,' she echoed.

He gasped and slammed his hands over his cheeks. He turned to get away from her. But there was nowhere to go. He tried to slide his body past her but she loomed ever closer.

'Together … forever.'

Frederick lunged past her but he slipped and fell over the side of the tower. He screamed as he fell. Then he landed. His blood splashed the grass and flowed towards the notice board.

If only Frederick had looked closer. He would have seen his name on the sheet of first-class degrees. But the pin from the second-class sheet was stuck through it. He just hadn't seen it. It was a tragedy.

Room twenty-one and the Black Staircase are said to be haunted by the ghosts of Isabella and Frederick to this day. She can be seen gliding up and down the stairs in her grey cloak. He can be heard pacing and sobbing in his room. They really did end up together forever in Durham Castle.

23

THE GIANTS OF COUNTY DURHAM

Long ago, when giants roamed Count Durham, there were two that lived over in Weardale. One at Stanhope and one at Frosterley. The Stanhope Giant was a vast, towering and muscle-bound beast covered in thick, black and coarse hair. The Frosterley Giant was lean and lithe with wiry and sinuous arms. The two were always bickering and fighting, mainly about whose land the dales where.

'This is my land!' bellowed the Stanhope Giant, 'I was here first!'

'Nonsense!' shouted back the Frosterley Giant, 'I'm as old as the land itself! I was here first!'

'You just keep off my deer!' snarled the Stanhope Giant, 'They're mine!'

'Yours?' snorted the Frosterley Giant. 'This is my hunting ground!'

On and on it went. The people of the villages were terrified that the giants might begin fighting and their homes would be trampled on. The giants exchanged insults and threats. They stamped their feet and shook their fists.

'Bollihope Common!' shouted one.

'You're the one who's common!'

'No! It's a place!'

'So what?'

'So we settle this there!'

'Oh yeah?'

'Yeah!'

'Right then, Bollihope Common it is!'

With that, the giants turned and thundered their way back to their homes to collect their clubs.

The people of Stanhope and Frosterley had heard every word of course and both villages were eager to see who would win.

A crowd of excited people from both places had gathered, at a safe distance from the common, on the nearby moorland.

Soon enough the ground began to tremble and shake. First arrived one giant and then the other. They carried with them great wooden clubs made from ancient oak trees from the nearby forest.

'You ready, little one?' goaded the Stanhope Giant.

But while he waited for a reply, the lean, swift Frosterley Giant lunged at him with his club and thrust it straight into the bulkier giant's belly. There was a blast of hurricane wind that slammed into the spectators, making them fall to the ground, as the Stanhope Giant exhaled long and hard from the blow.

He soon righted himself and hammered his own club into the ground, missing the other giant's toes by mere inches. The ground trembled, trees quivered and animals fled in terror. The giants swung their clubs at one another. They kicked, punched and swore.

On and on the battle went but at last both giants were tiring. With one last effort they smashed their clubs upon each other's skulls.

There was a terrible crunching noise and both giants fell to the floor together.

The dales folk ran over to see if either had survived the last dreadful blow but there on the ground were not two giants, but rather a vast pile of stones that *resembled* two giants slumped upon one another.

The people of Stanhope and Frosterley gave each other a cheery wave and returned to their villages. They were free of both beastly giants and decided that they were quite happy with the outcome. Not a stone was moved or lifted from that place and the locals call that pile of stones 'The Lang Men of Bollihope' to this day.

Weeks passed and the people of Weardale thought that their giant days were over. But they felt the familiar tremor upon the ground. They poured out of their houses to see not two, but three giants striding towards them. The terrified villagers raced back inside to hide under their tables and beds.

'Don't be scared!' called one giant.

'We're just visiting!' another added.

'Our cousins live here!' the third bellowed.

A little girl peered through closed curtains. She thought that the giants certainly looked friendly enough. Not like those last two.

'I'm Cor!'

'I'm Ben!'

'I'm Con!'

The girl made up her mind. She walked past her parents cowering under the kitchen table and opened the door.

'Hello,' she said in a small voice.

'Hello!' the giants called as one.

Their smiles were as huge as the hills.

'I'm afraid there was a fight,' the girl began.

The giants squatted down to hear the tragic tale.

'They always did have tempers.' Cor said, shaking his huge head.

'Always getting at each other,' Ben said sadly.

'Be best go back home then,' Con added grimly.

The girl waved goodbye as the three giant brothers strode over the land. Each footstep cleared the length of a farmer's field and soon they could no longer be seen.

The giants lived in the hills of Consett and made it back to their homes in mere minutes. They were surprised to see an old woman waiting for them.

'Hello!' the giants called to her.

The old woman stood up.

'I am the wise woman of Wolsingham,' she croaked.

'Hello!' they said again.

'I am here to tell you of a prophecy.'

The giant brothers were very intrigued and squatted to hear more.

'When the Long Men of Weardale turn to stone,

When the giants of Consett return home,

That is when the Hammer of Howden is given,

Born from fire and ice made clear through a vision.'

The giants noticed that the old woman was sitting on a huge hammer. It suddenly glinted in the sunlight.

'Is that for us?' asked Cor.

'It's a blacksmith's hammer!' Ben said, smiling.

'Us? Smithies?' Con asked.

The old woman stood up.

'You will make the finest swords and armour that the county has ever seen!' she declared, smiling. 'You will use the hills as anvils!'

The giants smiled at one another.

'But, the prophecy has a warning!'

'What is it?' they asked.

'The Hammer of Howden must be shared,

Its unique power is unimpaired.

But if it ever falls to the ground

Its wielders will never again be found.'

The wise woman of Wolsingham let this news sink in for a few moments.

'Once you pick this hammer up. It must never touch the earth.'

The three brothers looked at one another again.

Cor shrugged. Ben smiled. Con nodded.

Seemingly satisfied, the old woman waved and walked away leaving the giants to ponder the hammer.

'Shall I pick it up?' asked Cor.

'Once it's up. It stays up.' warned Ben.

'How will we sleep?' wondered Con.

The three sat down making the ground shake a little. They all stared at the hammer.

'I've always fancied being a blacksmith.'

'Me too.'

'Me three.'

They laughed and grinned.

'Go on then,' said Con.

'Pick it up,' nodded Ben.

Cor stood up and rubbed his chin. He then scooped up the hammer and held to the sun.

'It's so light!' he said. 'Here! Catch!'

He threw the hammer to Ben.

'Careful!' shouted Con. 'You drop that and we're done for!'

Ben laughed and threw the hammer to him.

'You're right!' Con said full of wonder. 'It really is light.'

'How will we sleep though?' Ben asked.

'We'll take turns.' Cor said.

Con nodded.

'Good plan.'

That night, none of the brothers slept. They talked and planned how they would work. They discussed who would make the fire, who would strike the metal on the hill anvils, who would hold the metal steady, where they would get the best materials from and all manor of other things until it was morning again.

The trio soon became masters of their craft. The hammer would be passed between them. They made the most exquisite helmets and intricately crafted shields. For ones so big their work was delicate and filled with minute detail.

As they only had the one hammer between them, they passed it from one to another. They soon found their favourite hills for anvils. Cor's was in Lanchester, Ben's was in Consett and Con's was in Shotley Bridge. So confident had they become with the feather-light hammer that they would hurl it to one another when they heard a whistle. The hammer would fly through the air making a humming sound. Each giant would whistle, hear the humming and get ready to catch.

So the giants made their living. Their work became famous across the county and beyond. Even the king ordered some to be made for the royal armouries.

The years passed.

The giants were busy, contented and fulfilled by their work. But age affects us all. Even giants. Eventually their eyes were not what they once were. They found that they had to listen for the hum of the hammer rather than see it race towards them.

On one winter's day, when the sun was low in the sky by mid-afternoon, Cor heard his brother Ben whistle for the hammer. He launched it and knew it was a bad throw. It had just slipped from his fingers a fraction too late. Ben heard the hum of the approaching hammer. He misjudged the noise and only just caught the tip of the handle in his hand. To stop himself from letting it slip, he launched the hammer up into the air towards Con.

'The hammer's coming Con!' he bellowed.

Con turned and heard the hum fast approaching.

'I haven't asked for it!' he called back.

The hammer came in, too fast. It bounced on Con's palms and slammed to the floor.

At soon as the hammer fell to the earth there was a flash of blinding white light. The hammer and the three giants instantly disappeared.

But, in the place named Howden, there is a long, large valley where the hammer once fell. That is the only trace left of the giant brothers of Consett.

24

THE BATTLE OF NEVILLE'S CROSS

John De Coupland nervously paced the gardens of Crook Hall. Peter Del Croke had very kindly invited the knight to rest at his beautiful home before riding to Neville's Cross the next day to fight an invading Scottish army led by their king himself. He knew that the English archers were the best in the world but he also knew that the Scottish were a formidable foe of skilled warriors.

Darkness would soon descend. The last light of the sun crept through the tangles of ivy. He sat down beside a curious statue that looked like a fairy. He sighed deeply.

'My father wishes to know if you'll dine with us,'

John turned and saw the most beautiful girl he had ever seen in his life. Her thick auburn hair fell in loose curls around her perfectly formed face. Eyes that seemed to alternate between green and grey smiled at him. Her full lips hid perfect white teeth. He could not speak. She held her hands and bowed her head slightly, waiting for an answer.

At last he stood and said, 'You must be Joan.'

She nodded shyly and blushed a little.

'I'm John,' he said taking a step towards her.

'I know.'

She blushed a little more.

'So will you be joining us?' she said a little too quickly.

'Yes. Yes, of course. Let me escort you back to the house.'

John and Joan walked and talked. She was the perfect distraction from what lay ahead.

Sleep did not come easily that night. John had seen vicious, bloody battles abroad and knew of the horrors of war. His dreams were haunted by visions of battlefields and crows. He heard his horse clopping on the cobblestones the next morning. He knew it was time.

'It is the thirteenth of October in the year of our lord 1346,' he said as he stood. 'My life is in God's hands.'

His horse was saddled and his armour was strapped upon his body. John gave thanks to his host and trotted down the hill towards the path that led to Neville's Cross. He suddenly remembered that he had not said goodbye to Joan. He cursed himself and vowed that if he survived the battle then he would get to know the girl a lot better. With the permission of her father of course.

Lost in thoughts of her face and voice, he soon drew his attention back to the day at hand when he heard the ocean of noise ahead. A vast army of English knights and archers had gathered on a field. They were splitting into three sections and organising themselves into a defensive position. This was the superior place to fight and John let out a long sigh of relief. He trotted over to the back of the middle section.

'John!' bellowed a familiar voice. 'Just in time! They're approaching!'

'I wouldn't miss it, Sir Thomas,' laughed John.

'Join me,' Thomas laughed back. 'We need fighting men like you in our battalion.'

John trotted over and saw the Scottish army in the distance.

'We heard of their attack at Kirk Merrington,' Thomas continued. 'Hence us calling in all local fighting men to this location. Did you rest nearby?'

'Aye,' answered John, 'Crook Hall.'

Thick coils of rolling fog lay between the English and Scots. The smoky fingers crept between the horses' legs of both battalions.

'It's only the weather that saved the day at Kirk Merrington,' said Thomas. 'Let's hope it helps today.'

The Scots stood fast at Bearpark. Their army standing stock-still and staring at the English. Neither army moved. Neither army spoke. That is until King David II of Scotland shouted,

'Make my breakfast!'

Pages scurried to make a fire and set to cooking their king a feast.

'I'll eat it when I have slain every English man at the point of my sword.'

The Scottish army laughed.

At this, the English archers stepped forward. They put swallow-tail arrows upon their yew bows and sent the spiralling arrows flying towards their enemy. The swallow-tail arrowheads were named after their design. Their curved wing tips made the arrows spin as they were shot, making their attack range vast. The English had aimed at the Scottish horses' legs to bring down the knights on top of them.

Next, the English archers let loose hundreds of armour-piercing needle bodkin arrows. Many men fell before even setting foot onto the battlefield.

'First division!' bellowed the king. 'Attack!'

A column of Scottish knights galloped into action. They were soon followed by a second division led by King David himself. Then went the third.

The English had divided themselves into three also. The first division of Scots clattered into the first of the English with screams and shouts. The clash of metal on metal and hooves on soil could be heard all around.

The Archbishop of York blessed the second division then led them into the fray himself with a mighty mace wielded in his hand.

'There's the third trumpet!' shouted Thomas. 'Charge!'

John had not heard the other trumpets as the noise of battle was so invasive. He drew his sword and galloped with his comrades. Sir Thomas led the third battalion round the back of all three Scottish battalions. They forced their enemy to close its ranks into one another. Sword swinging, John slammed into the enemy. Shields were dented, armour was punctured, swords were broken. Men screamed and men fell. Blood ran red.

In no time, another trumpet was sounded. It was the trumpet of the Scots; a call for retreat. So great was the loss from the archers' initial attack that the Scots stood no chance on the battlefield.

The third division of Scots, who were the last to join the battle, left first. The other two battalions, hearing the trumpet, were in chaos. Some left, some did not. King David's battalion headed in multiple directions. In the confusion, the king was abandoned. He managed to escape the fray but was alone.

Then, the English trumpets sounded out. A great cheer from the English battalions went up and weapons were lowered. The Scots could be seen running from Neville's Cross towards Bearpark and into the welcoming fog.

'The king has not been found!' shouted Sir Thomas. 'Find the king!'

John furrowed his brow. Everyone would be looking for the king. If he had not retreated with his army, where would he be able to hide? John's eyes scanned the landscape. There were no buildings. There was no shelter. Fields, hedgerows, river. The river Browney. That was it.

He turned his horse and galloped at speed towards a small stone bridge. Stopping his horse atop the bridge he scanned the river each on each side. Perhaps the king would be hiding among the bulrushes on one side, but no. Perhaps beneath the branches of a willow on the other.

Then John saw a reflection in the water.

He leaped down from his horse then jumped over the side of the bridge. Landing with a mighty thud and splash in the shallow water he looked upon King David II beneath the bridge.

The king leaped to his feet. He had dropped his weapon during the escape from the battlefield but still had his heavy gauntlets which could be used as weapons.

John pointed his sword at the king.

'You are my prisoner. I am —'

Before the words could come to fruition, the king knocked the sword to the side with one hand and slammed his fist into the

English knight's face. John fell back into
the water. Several teeth fell from his
mouth. He started to laugh.

'What're you laughing at?'
demanded the king, 'I've just
knocked your teeth out!'

John stood up and spat more teeth
into the water.

'You've just knocked my teeth out,' he
guffawed, 'But I've just captured a king! I'll
be rich!'

Scooping up his sword he held it out
towards the king's neck.

'John!' laughed Thomas from atop the bridge. 'You did it!'
More English knights arrived and King David II was tied with
ropes. Led by John, the knights made the long journey to London
where the king would be held at the Tower. John De Coupland was
given a handsome reward from Edward III for capturing the king.

The first thing he did once he had collected his money was head
straight back to Crook Hall. As soon as he arrived he asked Peter
Del Croke if he could marry his daughter. The father said yes and
then so did his daughter. Joan Del Croke and John De Coupland
were married and decided to move into Crook Hall some years
later in 1360. It was there that the knight who had captured a king
lived with the love of his life happily ever after.

25

DOBBIE AND CLOGGY

Maggie Brook was seeing her father home. She walked with him arm in arm over the moors towards the village of Shotton. A curved moon hung in the sky and the branches of the trees in the distance seemed to be scratching at the air in the wind.

'Its an eerie night,' puffed her father, coils of steam escaping his mouth like a train.

'Aye, that it is,' sighed Maggie.

She and her father now lived on their own since Maggie's mother had died a few years earlier. Her brother had gone to work for the East India Trading Company. She didn't know where he currently was.

Maggie now often walked her father home from the alehouse so that he would not fall down a quarry or get stuck in a peat bog.

It was as they saw their home in the distance that they noticed something unusual. It was a white figure that seemed to float upon the air. It was sliding across the moors towards then unnaturally fast.

'Damn my eyes,' her father had said. 'What is that?'

Maggie could not answer. She didn't know.

The white figure drew nearer. Maggie and her father held onto each other tightly.

Suddenly the figure was upon them. It was a huge white goose that did not walk or fly, but rather hovered in mid-air. It opened its beak and let out a most unnaturally loud shriek. It made the pair double over and cover their ears. Their eyes closed until the terrible sound was over.

When they opened their eyes, the goose was gone.

'It's like the white dog,' Maggie whispered.

'What was that?' her father asked, not hearing what she'd said.

'I don't know,' Maggie said in hurried tones. 'Let's get you home.'

The pair went back to their house. Once her father was in bed, Maggie sat staring into the flames of the fire. She was lost in thoughts about her mother. A white dog had appeared on the moors the night her mother had died. It too had floated towards her like some ghostly apparition and screamed at her when it got close, then disappeared.

The scream had been neither dog nor human. It was an unearthly thing.

She checked on her father every hour that night. Each time, it was the same, he snored throatily and all was well.

In the morning, as she made breakfast, she called for him to come into the kitchen for his porridge. But he did not.

She raced to his bedroom and found him quite dead beneath the covers. How could this have happened? He was snoring not an hour earlier!

At the funeral, she told her aunt about the white dog and now the white goose.

'It's a dobbie,' her aunt had told her. 'Nothing to be scared off. Dobbies warn you when someone is about to die.'

Maggie then lived by herself. She became a loner and spent hours looking out of her window across the moors for signs of a white phantom floating over the rough landscape.

Years passed.

On one cold winter's morning, Maggie was collecting the firewood that had been stacked by her front door by a kind neighbour. She was holding two armfuls and was about to go back inside when suddenly a white bird fluttered in the sky above her. It seemed to drift like a handkerchief on the wind rather than actually fly. The feathers were a glowing white. It made its slow descent and landed on the logs that Maggie carried.

It then shrieked and howled.

Maggie dropped the logs. She clasped her hands onto her ears. Involuntarily she squinted her eyes firmly shut. When she opened them the white bird had gone.

Hours later, there was a heavy knocking upon her door. She knew what the news would be and she was right.

Maggie went to her aunt's funeral three days later. She delivered the eulogy wearing the black dress that she seemed to live in these days. When she returned home she sighed sadly and closed the door. But as she turned around the most alarming sight met her.

A white donkey was standing in the living room. It looked at her with wide, knowing eyes. The white fur seemed to glow in the gloom of the room. White, wide teeth were revealed as it opened its mouth.

Maggie's hands were already clasped upon her ears but she forced herself to keep her eyes open. The donkey brayed a high-pitched squealing screech. It went on and on.

Maggie watched as the creature closed its mouth and then disappeared in a flash of blinding white light. She knew that this must be her brother.

Several days later the news arrived by telegram that her brother was indeed missing in India, presumed dead. She didn't presume. She knew.

That very night, Maggie made her decision to leave Shotton. There were too many memories that stung. She knew that the dobbie meant her no harm but she did not want to see it again.

In only a matter of weeks Maggie's bags were packed, the cottage sold and she was seated on a coach bound for the other side of Durham. She was heading for the little village of Staindrop. She was to have her lodgings at a public house where she would work as a cleaner and cook. Maggie had her own money from the sale of the cottage but she wanted to be busy. She wanted to leave all this death and strangeness behind her.

She settled in in no time. The landlady and Maggie became good friends, talking each night, once the villagers had left the ale-house, until the early hours of the morning.

'Have you ever had anything strange happen to you?' the landlady asked one night.

'Strange, how?' Maggie had warily asked.

'Ghostly,' came the reply.

'Why do you ask?'

'There have been occasions that people have *seen* things here at the public house. Heard them too.'

'Like what?'

'A ghostly figure banging and stomping on the stairs.'

'Does it mean any harm?' asked Maggie.

'None at all,' laughed the landlady, 'But it sends most to pack their bags and off they go!'

'Not me,' declared Maggie.

'I hope not, but we'll see.'

The next evening, the landlady asked Maggie to go up into the attic where she stored the dried foods to see if there were any onions.

Maggie made her way to the top floor but as she was on the final, narrow, wooden staircase she heard an almighty banging on either side of her feet. It was as if someone was wearing Dutch wooden clog shoes and was running up and down the stairs. First they ran to her left, passed her down the stairs, and then to the right, back up the stairs.

Maggie stood stock still for a moment. Then at last she said,

'Hello, Cloggy!'

The banging stopped instantly.

Maggie went into the attic, collected the onions and made her way back down the stairs. Later that night, Maggie told the landlady what had happened and what she had said.

'Ha!' laughed the landlady. 'That's the way to deal with ghosts and no two ways about it!'

The pair laughed and laughed.

'Cloggy' appeared to Maggie many more times but each time a racket was made, the ghost was quieted with a simple greeting. The girl and the ghost were what you might even call friendly. Her experiences with the dobbie of Shotton had perhaps made the girl more sensitive towards the plight of the paranormal.

Maggie spent the rest of her days living in Staindrop. But the villagers say that the night before she died at a ripe old age, a glowing white cow was seen standing on the village green letting out the most horrific howling any of them had ever heard before.

St Godric

Godric sat and smiled. He felt the bobbing of the waves upon the side of the ship. He had done well. His parents, Ailward and Edwenna, would be proud. He had had the most humble of beginnings in Walpole, in Norfolk. Now he travelled the world as a merchant and trader. His eyes scanned the deck. Below, in the cargo, were large pots of spices. They would sell for a vast amount of money.

The sun cheered Godric further as they sailed on. He had heard that the kingdom of Northumberland had rich trading places. He would start there and see how he got on.

The journey was long but peaceful. When Godric arrived in Northumberland he began his many meetings with the local traders. In no time at all, the spices were sold and he was a wealthy man.

The trading had gone quicker than he had imagined, so Godric had a little free time on his hands. He asked here and there about where to visit, and everyone spoke of the beauty of the island of Lindisfarne.

Godric decided to spend the day there. He walked onto the island at low tide. The reputation of the island was not exaggerated. Arrowhead formations of geese sliced through the air above. Haunting seal-song greeted him as he walked over the glowing yellow sand. The sea seemed to sparkle as if jewels encrusted the surface of the water.

Godric spent a pleasant day strolling around. Then he saw another island. It was much smaller than Lindisfarne and as the tide was so far out, he could walk over the smooth, sleek pebbles to it. The island was covered in fine grass more green than Godric had ever seen before. He sat upon it and closed his eyes.

He was at that moment more alone than he had been in years. No bustling markets or traders. No busy sailing vessels. He loved it. He loved the tranquillity. He felt so comfortable. Life was good. Just then, he felt a warm gush of air fall upon him.

He opened his eyes and saw the figure of a man bathed in golden light. The figure wore a bishop's mitre and held a shepherd's crook. Stepping forward, the man wore a kindly expression. The light radiated from him. He sat beside Godric and smiled.

'Who are you?' asked the bewildered entrepreneur.

'I am Cuthbert,' the glowing man answered. 'I once lived here but my home is now in Durham.'

The unlikely pair spent the afternoon talking. The tide came in trapping them both on the small island. Neither minded. They were engrossed in conversation for hours and hours.

Eventually, Godric fell asleep on the curiously soft grass. When he awoke, Cuthbert was gone. But the words he had shared with Godric were not. He decided to be a trader no more. He wanted to be like Cuthbert and devote his life to serving God as a monk.

His life as a trader made him well qualified to travel. So Godric embarked on many journeys to Europe and North Africa. He sailed the whole of the Mediterranean spreading the word of God's love through Christianity. He spoke frequently of his encounter with Cuthbert and shared many of the wise things he had learnt from the saint. Godric spent years travelling from Spain to Morocco, then Egypt to Turkey, Algeria to Croatia to Albania to Tunisia to Libya.

Finally, he returned to England and sought out a hermit's life. He longed to live as Cuthbert did. He found a hermit called Aelric and spent two years living with and learning from the old man.

When Aelric died, Godric went travelling again. He had a final journey to the Holy Land of Jerusalem.

It was on this final journey that he had a vision from God. He was told to live as a hermit on the River Wear.

Godric returned home and travelled straight to Durham. There he had an audience with the Prince Bishop Ranulf Flambard. He asked if he could live at a place that would later be named Finchale. It was a deserted place by the river and the bishop agreed.

For over sixty years Godric lived at Finchale on the Wear. People visited him frequently to listen to his wise words or hear him preach. He had a particular fondness for animals, just as Cuthbert did. Pope Alexander III came to visit Godric and seek his wise council. As did Thomas Becket. His fame spread far and wide and people flocked to Durham to meet him. His fame did not just spread to the ears of man either. The devil himself heard of Godric's wisdom and virtue. So the devil decided to test Godric.

A traveller arrived in Finchale seeking food and shelter. Godric gave the man both and in return the man told Godric of a secret hoard of gold that was buried not far from there.

'Why don't you get it for yourself?' Godric had asked.

'You have shown me such kindness,' the man smiled earnestly, 'that you should have it. I was on my way to dig it up myself but I think that you are more deserving.'

'I have no need of money!' laughed Godric.

'No,' grinned the man, 'but the church does. Imagine what a hoard of gold could do for the church!'

That got Godric thinking. He had to agree that the man made a fair point. So directions were given and the man bade farewell.

Godric set off to retrieve the gold with a pickaxe and shovel. He began to break up the ground where the man had told him. He dug deep into the earth but there was no sign of treasure of any sort.

By the time he was neck deep under the earth, Godric was covered in dripping sweat.

'I'll go a little deeper but then no more,' Godric said to himself.

He hammered at the soil with the pickaxe then felt the earth shudder and shake beneath his feet. The ground then cracked open and Godric fell.

Down, down, down he tumbled, until at last he landed with a heavy thump upon the floor. He looked around. It was dark but he could make out eyes in the gloomy shadows. Lots of eyes. Beady, small and ink black. They peered at him. Then they began to chuckle and snort. Small figures scuttled towards him. They ignited flames from their clawed hands and laughed with glee at Godric's fright.

They slammed fireballs into the floor around him. They danced in circles jeering and guffawing.

'Godric set us free!' they chanted. 'Godric set us free!'

The impish creatures then poured out of the hole and onto the land beyond. Godric sat slumped upon the floor. What had he done?

The devil is a fiend and a liar. He sends the weak-minded to test those even weaker of mind. He had been tested. He had failed.

Godric climbed out of the dark and into the light. He knew that he had to be stronger than the prince of lies.

So the hermit began to take to wearing a very old and incredibly itchy sackcloth. He then wore a back plate and chest plate of heavy armour. When asked about the curious clothes Godric replied that the sackcloth shirt constantly itched him to remind him always to be aware of the devil's tricks. He also said that the armour was the heavy burden he had taken upon himself to serve God alone.

Godric knew that Cuthbert often spent hours submerged in the North Sea deep in prayer. The saint had told Godric when they met on Lindisfarne that this brought him closer not only to God, but nature and animals too. So, one day, Godric laid his clothes on the riverbank and submerged himself in the River Wear up to his neck.

It was while he shivered and prayed that the devil decided to visit Godric himself this time. He stood on the riverbank and shouted at the monk. But Godric ignored him. He stamped his foot and called out names. But Godric ignored him. The devil screeched and raged. Godric ignored him still.

The devil was so furious that he stole Godric's clothes and ran away laughing. But the monk simply kept on praying.

When he had finished, he calmly stepped out of the river and began to say prayers aloud. He prayed to St Anthony of Padua for the return of his lost clothes. His prayers were said with such passion and might that the devil was forced to put them back exactly where they were before. The devil was so furious that he stamped a cloven hoof upon the floor and disappeared in a puff of fire and brimstone.

The site of Godric's hermitage attracted a lot of animals to it. Like Cuthbert, he loved all creatures. One night, snakes slithered from the forest. Godric was sat warming himself by a roaring fire. The nest of snakes cautiously slid along the ground and waited.

'It's all right,' Godric said with his eyes closed, 'You can join me.' The snakes did not need telling twice. They approached the fire and basked in the orange glow. They stayed there all night then went off into the forest the next morning.

Godric awoke to the sound of a hunting horn. It blasted through the trees and into his ears. His brow furrowed. He did not like the sound of the hunt. He stood, sighed, and strolled down to the river for a drink.

Suddenly there was a crashing sound behind him. The hermit whirled around and saw a huge stag had burst through the trees. Steam poured from its mouth, its chest heaved up and down. A tongue lolled from its mouth. It was clearly exhausted.

'Come,' Godric said with arms outstretched as a gesture of peace, 'I'll hide you.'

The stag stepped forward, seeming to understand the words. Godric took a large sheet he had slept under.

'Kneel under this,' he said.

The stag bent its knees and lowered itself to the ground. Godric pulled the sheet over it. He then covered it with leaves and bracken. As he turned, the hunters arrived.

'Monk!' one barked. 'We've tracked a stag down here. Have you seen it?'

'Yes,' Godric answered smiling at them, 'he crossed the river, that way.'

He pointed to a shallow path in the Wear that led to the other side.

'He's a crafty one,' the hunter growled, 'he's trying to lose his scent.'

With that, the hunters splashed into the river and rode to the other side. Godric pulled free the sheet. The stag stood then lowered its antlers to Godric. The monk stroked the soft fur of the stag's head.

Then the stag trotted away in the opposite direction to the river. Godric watched him disappear into the dense forest.

That night, Godric sat by the fire again. This time snakes did not join him though. The devil watched him from between trees. He wanted revenge on the monk. The devil decided to transform himself into a fearsome wolf and padded slowly towards the fire.

'I see who you are,' Godric said without turning to look at the terrifying creature. 'You are not welcome by my fire.'

The devil-wolf snarled. Its red eyes glowed with fury. It howled and barked. Frothed and raged.

Godric just laughed and made the sign of the cross. This made the devil flee. But each night the devil returned to Godric. One night he was a hungry dog, another, a wild boar and on another, he was a sneaky fox. The monk saw through every disguise and sent the devil racing away upon saying a prayer or chanting the Trinitarian formula aloud.

It enraged the devil utterly. Here were all kinds of animals warming themselves by Godric's fire each night yet the monk saw through the devil's every transformation. No matter what animal the devil became, small or large, fierce or gentle, the monk just seemed to *know*.

Godric lived for many years down by the river. When he was an old man he had another visitor. In a glow of glorious white light the Virgin Mary appeared to Godric. She wore shining white and blue robes. She told Godric that she would always be with him in his times of need. She also taught him a song of consolation. This song, she told, him would forever banish the devil and dismiss any thoughts of temptation.

The devil never visited again after that day.

Before Godric died, he met with Reginald of Durham, who was a great composer. Godric shared his life story with the musician and four songs were written about the monk. They are oldest recorded composed pieces of music in England. They live on to tell the tale of one of the greatest saints that ever lived. Finchale Priory now stands at Godric's hermitage. This too serves as a monument to Saint Godric.

27

THE PEOPLE'S PIPER

The Lower Prison sits beside the River Wear under Elvet Bridge. It is now known as Jimmy Allen's Nightclub and Bar. It gets its name from the once famous piper who is now almost forgotten. Jimmy Allen was amazing at catching vermin. He would catch moles for the local farms in return for food and lodgings. Later, he would sell the moleskins at the market. He could also catch mice and rats like no other. He was an expert fisherman too. He settled for a while on the River Coquet where he got the job as 'water-keeper'. But he was a traveller and he loved his life on the road.

His vermin and fish-catching skills and fame were no match for his pipe-playing, however. Jimmy played the Northumbrian Border pipes and he could make the sweetest-sounding music you would ever hear. From the mournful and melancholy, to the cheery and chirpy. Everyone agreed that Jimmy Allen was a most gifted player.

He had been taught to play by his adoptive father, Wull Faa. The Faa clan was a group of Romany-Gypsy travellers who lived in the Cheviots in the Scottish Borders. The Faas found Jimmy as a young boy, roaming the Northumberland countryside, stealing food and living wild. They took him in and Wull Faa played his pipes by the fire every night.

Jimmy was hooked the second he heard them. He begged Wull to teach him and what a student he was! Jimmy practised morning, noon and night. So he grew up with the Faas and entertained *them* each night with tunes of old as well as new ones he had composed himself that day. Two of his pipe tunes he composed over those joyous nights were 'Salmon Tails up in the Water' and 'We'll A' to the Coquet and Woo'.

The Faas travelled the borders and over all of Northumberland. Jimmy's fame grew and he eventually became the official piper for the Countess of Northumberland. He was invited to play regularly at Alnwick Castle and there he won the hearts of the rich. He made influential friends. He was loved by all of the powerful Percy family. They created the role of Ducal Piper just for Jimmy – he became known as the 'Piper to the Countess'. He wore the Percy's Crusade Trophy upon his right arm wherever he went. This showed people that he was under the protection of the Percys, including the Countess.

The Countess had a special set of pipes made for him in Edinburgh. They were made of ivory and decorated with silver chains. With these pipes, Jimmy was invited to play at the coronation of George III. He had made it. He was the people's piper who played for royalty.

But Jimmy was wild. He loved drinking and he loved women. More often that not he loved the *wrong* women. He was always getting into scrapes of one kind or another with wives or rich husbands. The problem was that women loved him too. He was clever and witty. He made them laugh. But most of all, he dazzled them with his pipe music.

He also loved to gamble. Jimmy's gambling meant that he needed money fast, so he often talked his way into ladies' purses before charming his way to their beds. This often led to murderous husbands trying to track him down.

So Jimmy enlisted into both British and foreign armies. Once he was far enough away from the trouble, he would desert whatever army he was meant to be serving and move on to the next place.

He enlisted and deserted more times than he could count. But everywhere Jimmy travelled to, trouble travelled with him. Cattle stealing became another favourite pastime as it generated vast sums of money, which the piper would then gamble away.

Once, the roguish traveller made it to Edinburgh where he played his pipes up and down the Royal Mile. Enraged Scottish Pipers followed to break his pipes but Jimmy even won the hearts of these traditionalists. He showed them the pipes that had been made in their city then led them to tavern after tavern. They drank and played their music together all night long.

Jimmy married, not for the first time, in Edinburgh, but then got tired of his latest wife so went off to Dublin. There he fell in love with the city. He loved the people, the stories and the music. Yet even here, he got into bother with a rich lord's wife. He enlisted again and found himself sailing the seas with the Dutch East India Company. He went to the Baltic and to India but didn't actually perform any work duties for the company. He simply entertained with his pipes and got a free ticket to travel the world.

Finally, Jimmy longed for his English home. He missed the North East and the people. He found himself in Durham and loved it almost as much as he had Dublin. When the Percys heard of his return they invited him to play at both Alnwick and Warkworth Castle. Their piper had returned to them and it was time to celebrate. Jimmy wowed the crowds and all past misdemeanours were forgotten, briefly anyway.

For the piper could not change his ways.

He was arrested for stealing a horse from Durham. Apprehended in Jedburgh, the piper was taken back to Durham where he was convicted and held in the Lower Prison on the Wear. It was while here that he was finally sentenced to death. All of his past actions and crimes had come back to haunt Jimmy as an angry crowd had gathered and implored the judge for justice. Victims of his gambling, theft and adultery bayed for blood.

But Jimmy still had a lot of friends. Important friends. A petition was sent to London for the eyes of King George III only, requesting Jimmy's immediate release. But George III was unwell. He did not get to see the petition. The king's son, the Prince Regent, eventually saw the document. He remembered Jimmy from tales his father had told, so he signed the document and sent it back to the prison.

Jimmy was unwell himself though. In his seventy-seventh year the piper passed away. He died in his cell in the cold and the dark with the rats. The royal pardon arrived too late. It arrived four days after Jimmy Allen had died. He was buried in St Nicholas's Churchyard in Durham.

Some say though, that if you walk along the River Wear, near to where the piper died, you can hear the mournful pipes playing late at night.

28

Bridget and Bobby

Bobby Shafto's gone to sea,
Silver buckles at his knee;
He'll come back and marry me,
Bonny Bobby Shafto!
Bobby Shafto's bright and fair,
Panning out his yellow hair;
He's my love for evermore,
Bonny Bobby Shafto!

Dave Hart arrived in Durham full of expectation. He was young, talented and about to move into a castle. He was a percussion-ist and musician. A storyteller and raconteur. A spoon-carver. Bushcraft enthusiast. In short, he could turn his hand to most things.

Dave had heard of an artists' commune living in Brancepeth Castle. There were artists, musicians, potters and many more all living in affordable rooms thanks to the owner Margaret Dobson. She had bought the castle in the 1970s and had made it a home for herself, her family and her creative tenants. Dave had never felt more at home. He settled into his vast room and admired the four-poster bed and roaring open fire.

He would be happy here. He would be living with like-minded people in a county filled with history. He would study folklore and

mythology at the university. He would make a living doing what he loved on the side.

All went as planned but the room that Dave lodged in was difficult to keep warm. The fire devoured log after log, endlessly throughout the night. No matter what, Dave just could not keep that room warm. There was a permanent chill in the air that crept right into his very bones. He slept on the sofa, which he pulled next to the fireplace, yet even that made little difference.

The duvets, blankets, fleeces and throws were piled high upon him. And he shivered beneath.

All the while, Dave felt as if he was being watched. It was only a feeling but it was a very certain one.

One cold and sleepless night, he heard windows rattle. First one then another. Soon, all three large windows banged simultaneously. It sounded as if there were people outside hammering at the glass.

Dave slid from beneath his cavernous covers and cautiously crept to a window. He pulled the curtains to one side and peered into the darkness. The silhouettes of the trees indicated that it was a still and silent night with barely any wind at all. Yet the windows continued to bang and rattle.

'Stop,' he heard himself say.

Instantly, the windows stopped.

'That's better. Now, be good.'

Dave climbed back onto the sofa and fell into a deep sleep. No more noise was heard that night.

The cold gradually got worse. In the end, Dave could stand it no more. He took to sleeping in his van. It was warmer outside the castle than it was inside. After a few nights of this though, he grew tired of roughing it outside. He spoke to the other residents about the cold in the castle.

No one else experienced this in their rooms. It was only in his room. It was suggested that he should seek the advise of a psychic. As in many folk tales from County Durham, a wise woman could be the answer.

Dave made an appointment with a local woman who fitted the description. She asked him which room he was staying in at the castle.

'You know who used to live in that room, don't you?' the psychic had asked.

Dave shook his head.

'Bridget Bellasis.'

Dave looked blank.

'She was the fiancée of a member of parliament from County Durham. But this wretch went off and married Ann Duncombe. Bridget died of a broken heart two weeks after she heard the news. She died in the room where you now live.'

Dave's eyes widened.

'Who was the MP?' he asked.

'Went by the name of Bobby Shafto.'

The nursery rhyme crept its way into Dave's memory. He sang it several times over inside his head.

'We need to perform an exorcism in your room,' the psychic then said. 'We need to give Bridget the peace she deserves.'

Dave eventually agreed and the exorcism was arranged. The psychic and a priest arrived at the castle a few days later. Dave had taken to sleeping back in his room. It was still very cold but he somehow now felt a link to the ghost in his room. He felt sorry for her.

He looked on as the ritual was performed.

After the pair left. Dave sat on his sofa and looked into the fire. He felt a sad sense of loss. The room was never cold again after that night. The roaring fire rapidly filled the enormous room. Dave slept in his bed but his thoughts often returned to Bridget. He felt somehow attached to her. In Dave's own words he says,

'I felt she had nestled me into some kind of colluded warm and cosy dependency with her. Although it felt much fresher and new when she had gone, there was definitely a feeling of loss, like after you break up with someone. Sounds weird I know ....'

He missed her. But the ghost with the broken heart was gone.

Bobby Shafto's gone to sea,
Silver buckles at his knee;
He'll come back and marry me,
Bonny Bobby Shafto!
Bobby Shafto's bright and fair,
Panning out his yellow hair;
He's my love for evermore,
Bonny Bobby Shafto!

29

THE HIGH GREEN GHOST

Peg Powler is the hag of the River Tees. Mothers warned their children about her. But children seldom listen.

Andrew skipped to the riverbank. He skimmed stones over the sleek surface. He was getting good at it. He could manage seven skips at least, as long as the stone was right. The banks of the river near his village of Middleton in Teesdale had the perfect stones. They were smooth as silk and flat as pancakes. They fitted perfectly into your palm. It was all in how the stone was released. Andrew knew that.

He wanted to impress Fiona next door. He would practise a few more times then bring her down to the river to admire his stone-skipping skill. Collecting several suitable stones, he walked along the bank and found a nice deep section of the river. This was the perfect place for stone-skipping.

There was a cluster of rocks further upstream. There was a white foamy froth gathering on these.

Andrew stepped between some long, tall bulrushes and steadied his posture. All in the release. He breathed in deeply, closed his eyes for a moment to relax, and concentrated. Fiona would think he was amazing. None of the other boys could manage seven or eight skips.

Suddenly, he felt something grip his ankle. He looked down and dropped the stones.

A green hand was holding his leg. He screamed and tried to pull his leg away but the grip was firm. Another hand emerged. Some pondweed fell to one side of it as it raced to grab his other ankle. He tried to pull free of the hands but they yanked him forward and, with a jerk backwards, he fell to the floor. There was a light, dull thud as he landed on thick reeds. The hands pulled again and his feet were in the water. It was colder than ice. Andrew screamed and flailed his arms trying to get a better grip on the bulrushes he had just grabbed.

The hands were holding on even tighter now. Sharp nails cut the skin and drew blood. They were pulling him further into the river. He screamed again as his legs were now utterly submerged.

Then a face emerged from the dark waters. A tress crown rose first. It was made of both hair and reeds. Then the face. An impossibly ugly, green woman leered at the boy. She had huge, bulging fish like eyes. A bulbous nose was covered in warts but was sleek smooth like frog's skin. Long, lank black hair framed the grotesque portrait. Her smile was as wide as her face and revealed row after row of tiny, very sharp teeth. She gnashed these making the teeth grind upon one another. A thin, black, serpent tongue traced the lines of her lips.

Hysterically, Andrew fought to crawl back to the bank but the hag pulled him further in. With a plopping sound he was gone beneath the surface of the water. A few bubbles escaped his mouth then there was nothing.

His mother searched for him but she knew his fate. She knew he never listened to her. She knew that Peg Powler had eaten him up.

She was right.

The hag had finished her meal and sat in the river with her mouth wide open. The little fish that live in the Peg Powler's mouth were feeding on the bits of food that still clung to her teeth. This was a symbiotic relationship, as in return, these little fish kept her teeth sharpened.

There was a funeral but no body lay inside the coffin. Afterwards, when gathered in the alehouse to pay respects to the deceased, Andrew's mother spoke.

'We need to warn our children!' she said to the crowd. 'They *must* stay away from the river!'

Everyone agreed. They all said it was a tragedy.

'To us in Middleton in Teesdale she is the High Green Ghost,' Old Jennie croaked. 'To others she is Peg Powler. It is her that kills the little ones for her supper.'

'What are we to do then?' shrieked Andrew's mother.

'She has a warning sign,' Old Jennie croaked. 'It's plain to see, if you know what you're looking for.'

The crowd in the alehouse was silenced.

Old Jennie *knew* things.

'When the foam gathers on the rocks, these are Peg Powler's suds. It means she's foaming for food. She's hungry.

'When there's a pool of floating scum on the surface of the water, this is Peg Powler's cream. It means she's on the move. She's getting closer!'

The parents and other adults in the alehouse all nodded and whispered to one another. The children thought it exciting though. Fiona looked at her fiends. She mouthed the word,

'Outside.'

Soon, the children were gathered outside of the alehouse.

'Let's go down to the river,' Fiona said.

'Are you daft?' asked Robert. 'Why would we do that?'

'Andrew was my friend,' declared Fiona.

'Yeah, your boyfriend!' laughed Robert.

The others joined in with the laughter.

'Andrew was *our* friend,' Fiona said defiantly. 'We know about Peg Powler's ways now. There's enough of us. We should take our sticks and beat that old hag to death!'

No one said anything for a few moments. Fiona looked each child directly in the eyes until they nodded to her.

'That's agreed then,' she said, firmly. 'Riverbank. Five minutes.' The children raced off to gather their sticks. The first to the riverbank was Fiona. The others soon arrived after. There were five of them.

The children looked for any sign of the hag. They walked the bank first one way and then the other.

But there was no sign.

Eventually, downhearted, the five children returned home.

But Robert had other plans. He had heard the way Fiona had talked about Andrew. Robert needed to impress her himself. He needed her to feel that strongly about him. He would kill Peg Powler. He would do it on his own.

Later that night, Robert crept out of his house. He knew which stair creaked. He knew which door squeaked.

Collecting a lantern and a long stick, he made his way down to the riverbank. His eyes scanned the water. There was croaking from frogs and toads in every direction. A white slither of a moon was reflected off the oil-black water.

He set the lantern down beside some bulrushes. It cast an eerie yellow glow from the candle that made shadows dance upon the water's surface. Prodding the ground with a stick to make sure it was firm, he stepped right beside the river. Robert waited.

There was nothing.

He was tired and feeling impatient. Then he stepped into the shallow water of the bank. He waited again.

He waded into the middle of the river. The water was freezing but he didn't mind. When he brought Peg Powler's body back into the village he would be a hero.

Robert didn't notice the pool of scum that floated on the surface of the water in front of him. He waited with stick in hand ready to dash the head of any attacker that may approach.

Robert just then realised that the chorus of croaking had stopped. He looked around him. It was utterly and completely silent. He licked his lips. Uncertainty began to creep around the edges of his mind. Perhaps this was not such a good idea. He turned and waded towards the bank of the river.

There was a sudden splashing and Robert was beneath the water. Hungry little teeth chomped at his neck. He gurgled and spat. He splashed and was then still.

In the cold and dark he was devoured.

Peg Powler then sat in the River Tees and let the little fish clean her teeth. That is where she sits to this day. She is hungry. She is always hungry.

30

The Brawn of Brancepeth

In the land of Ferie, now named Ferryhill, there was a rather unwelcome but regular visitor. It was a huge and monstrous boar. The boar would travel far for its food. Its home was the woods at Brandon Hill.

The locals called it 'brawn' as it would come down 'Brawn Path' looking for juicy roots or ripe acorns that had tumbled to the ground. If anyone got in its way then the boar would snort and rage, it would mangle and maim.

Parents would warn their children to stay out of the brawn's way, but children get distracted by their games. It was when one of these children was attacked and killed that the people of Ferie called upon the help of the Brancepeth Knights. A lot of the knights were off fighting abroad but those that remained gladly agreed to help. The Ferie people also went to the monks of Merrington and asked for them to pray for the brave warriors.

These knights left Brancepeth Castle and galloped along to Brawn Path. They searched the lane and the woods that lined either side of it but none of them could find any trace of the beast. A few of the horses got stuck in the marshes and after a long and frustrating day the knights decided that enough was enough.

'We've frightened the brawn away!' they declared to the crowd gathered at Ferie, 'It is gone!'

A great cheer went up into the air. The people were satisfied. The knights had done their job. They thanked them and they thanked the monks. Life would return to normal for the good folk of Ferie.

But it did not.

A forester was out gathering firewood when he stumbled across the brawn. It was digging for truffles when the man saw it. The brawn sniffed at the air. Its cavernous nostrils snorted angrily when it caught the scent of then man.

The forester was frozen to the floor momentarily. He looked at the brawn with fearful eyes. The brawn stared back in rage.

The man turned and ran. The brawn gave chase. He was upon the forester in seconds. The hooves slammed the man to the floor. The savage tusks ripped and tore at the flesh. The brawn stamped and stomped, gored and gouged. Even when the man was dead the beastly brawn continued its deadly assault.

News of the forester's grizzly death reached the people of Ferie and they went back to Brancepeth Castle to plead for help. Roger De Ferie had just returned from the Crusades. When he heard that his home was under attack he insisted that he should undertake the quest alone.

But Roger did not send for his squire to fetch his armour. Instead he saddled his horse and trotted away from the castle towards his old home of Ferie. He tied the horse to a large oak tree at Cliff Cross then made his way to Brawn Path.

He smoothed soil over his skin. He rubbed the earthy loam all over his arms, legs and face to mask his scent. Then he lay down upon the ground and waited. He watched and he waited. He waited the entire day and at last the brawn came lumbering along.

It was a vast beast, covered in thick grey and brown fur. Each hair was as thick as a man's finger and ended in a needlepoint tip. The tusks were yellowed and curved. Its hooves were still encrusted with the blood of the forester.

Roger held his breath.

He watched the leaves and stones bounce from the floor with every step that the brawn made. Crouching lower, Roger held his breath.

The brawn went off down the path and headed for the woods at Mainsforth. The knight heaved himself up and followed at a safe distance. Once the brawn had gone to its lair deep inside the woods, Roger set to work.

He had brought only two things with him; a sword and a spade. He began digging and kept it up all night. The sweat dripped from his forehead and onto the moonlit ground. The hole he dug was as deep as a grave and as wide at the road. He used his spade to climb up from the pit then drew his sword.

Roger hacked down boughs and branches. Then he placed the longer and stronger branches over the huge hole. The leafier, more slender branches he put on top. He then used the spade to cast a thin layer of soil over the top of the lot. In the darkness, the path looked just as it had before he had begun but Roger hoped that in the morning it would still look as solid. He hoped that the brawn would be fooled.

The trap had been set.

Now he had to wait again. But he did not have to wait long for his digging had taken up most of the night. The glowing morning light replaced the gloom of the night. The low sun sent white light over the land.

The trap now looked less camouflaged. Roger shook his head. He should have added more soil. He peered down the path and decided to add more straight away before the brawn appeared. But as he threw the first clump of soil he heard a sniffling and snorting. Whirling around he slammed his body into the undergrowth. The bracken and thorns stabbed at him but he did make a sound.

He crouched low and waited. Anticipation fizzed in the air. Goosebumps irritated his skin. He said silent prayers.

The brawn came lumbering along. It stopped and sniffed the air.

Roger pursed his lips.

The brawn carried on up the path towards the trap. It stopped again and sniffed.

The knight wished he had replaced the soil over his sweat sodden face.

The brawn then resumed its painfully slow journey. Then it neared the trap.

With teeth gritted, Roger prayed again.

There was a deafening splintering of wood as the brawn fell into the pit with a thunderous thud. It shrieked and squealed in rage. It charged and banged off the sides of its pit. Roger knew that he had to be quick. He knew that the mighty beast would slam at the soil and be able to dig itself to freedom. He snatched up his sword and sprinted to the raging beast.

The knight plunged the sword down and into the brawn's skull. Its squealing was suddenly silenced. The creature went rigid for a second and when Roger pulled free the sword, it slumped into the pit, dead.

Roger de Ferie was victorious. His village home celebrated for weeks hailing him as a hero.

Many years later, when Roger died an old man, he was buried at Cliff Cross, near the Brawn's Path. That place is now known as Cleves Cross. It is there that a stone in the shape of a cross stands. It bears a carving of a sword on one side and a spade on the other as a memorial to great hero from Ferryhill.

31

THE DURHAM PUMA

The Kellas Cat prowled the riverbank in Scotland. Her yellow, slit-eyes narrowed as she watched the sleek salmon glide through the dark water. The spectral feline padded a paw into the oily water and scooped up a writhing fish. She devoured the flesh silently and watched the landscape. Her midnight fur swayed slightly in the wind. She had to feed more often than ever now that she carried young in her womb.

Her litter was born on a cold winter's morning. The mewing trio feasted hungrily on their mother's milk. They too were huge and black. When the kittens grew into cats, they parted company. The Kellas Cat is a solitary creature.

Years passed.

The mother Kellas died in the highlands of Scotland. From the litter, the eldest cat was caught in a snare and killed by a game-keeper in Revack Lodge on the River Spey while it hunted for its favourite fish. The middle cat was caught in the lowlands of Aberdeen. But the youngest cat travelled across the borders and into England. It arrived in County Durham where it found a large hunting ground.

It was a huge beast, much larger than its mother and siblings. The smooth, glossy feline was more the size of a big cat, like a puma. It did not share its family's appetite for fish but rather preferred the flesh of rabbits, hares and lambs.

This Kellas Cat would move from Consett, through to Spennymoor, then to Shincliffe and Pittington. It was clever. The cat never stayed in one place for too long. It knew that humans could catch and kill it. It was stealthy and wary.

On one summer's night, Katherine was walking down the dip from Sherburn and up the dip towards Durham. The sun was low. Shafts of yellow light blinded her as she passed a farm. She could smell the rich fragrant flowers all around. It tickled her nostrils and made her sneeze. She chuckled to herself.

Then she heard a noise that made her stop with an abrupt halt. It was a most terrible bleating sound. She squinted into the strange light of dusk and peered into a field. The lambs were running way from something. She stepped forward and gasped. A huge black beast had set upon a lamb and was busy tearing through its neck. A crimson wave splashed onto the green field.

'Hey!' she yelled, 'Hey! Stop!'

Before she knew what she was doing, Katherine squeezed herself between the barbed wire fence of the field. The lifeless body of the lamb, with an almost severed head, slumped to the floor making a terrible squelching sound.

The black beast crouched low and growled at the woman. It was a cat but larger than anything that Katherine had ever seen before. The yellow eyes narrowed and a lip snarled revealing long white sabre like teeth. The cat's tail swished menacingly and it crept towards her. Katherine gulped and stepped backwards. She felt the dull stab of the fence at her back.

The claws of the cat sunk into the soft grass and it roared loudly.

Katherine closed her eyes. She waited for the pain of the pounce. She clenched her fists and unclenched them again. She knew that this was the end.

But nothing happened.

Her eyes opened slightly. She winced a little waiting for the attack.

The cat had gone. So had the body of the lamb.

A red trail led away from the field and towards a cluster of trees in the distance.

Katherine let out a long, loud sigh. She squeezed herself through the fence and ran back to her home. She called the police and described her almost fatal encounter with a puma in a field in Durham. She was not believed. But reports of the large cat go on being given even to this day. So the next time you go for a stroll along the numerous beautiful country lanes of Durham just watch out for a large black beast. Who knows if it has yet found a taste for human flesh?

32

THE LAMBTON WORM

John Lambton was reckless. John Lambton was wild. John Lambton was young.

His parents were wealthy and, like a lot of rich families, had sent their son first to be a page then to be a squire and finally to be a knight. He had trained to wrestle, joust and fence. He had learnt how to dance and write poetry. He wore the colours of the Templars, red and white, to represent strength and peace. The colours of Sunderland to this day. He bore the Holy Cross to show his Christian beliefs. Even the great helm he now wore was emblazoned with the cross of Jesus. His quest to the Holy Land with the other knights was to spread the word of God.

But, before all of this, John Lambton would not do as his parents asked. He would run away from the castle as often as he could. He would fight the boys in the villages around the castle who called him spoilt and rich. He would spend hours down by the river fishing when he was meant to be attending dinners in the great hall or masses in the chapel.

It was during a mass on a Sunday morning, when John Lambton was sitting by the River Wear, that the terrible tale began. The boy had run off when his parents called him to put on his finest robes that day and had collected his fishing gear as he went.

He sat, hidden by bulrushes and reeds, and cast his line into the fast-flowing water and waited. There were salmon that raced the currents in those dark waters. He had caught them before. A smug smile of satisfaction was now sitting comfortably upon his face. A sigh, long and deep, escaped through wide lips. It was then that his fishing rod twitched and shook. John Lambton reeled in the line to find nothing on his hook. He grumbled and cast the line again. As soon as the bait hit the water, the line and rod vibrated in the boy's hand.

With a befuddled expression on his face, John reeled it in. Again, there was nothing upon his hook. So for a third time he cast his line.

The fishing rod buzzed. He turned the line quickly and angrily. When he saw that there was still nothing caught on his hook the boy bellowed,

'I curse you, river!'

He stood up and shook his fist.

'I curse everything in the river!'

He stamped his foot upon the soft mud of the bank. He looked at the church beyond the water.

'And I curse everyone in the church too!'

The sky darkened. Ominous black clouds crowded together, bustling to block out the sun. The boy cast a dubious look at them and cast his line into the dark depths of the river. He shuddered. A chill raced down his spine. He sat and pulled his cloak around him.

The fishing rod buzzed rhythmically.

He stared at it with wide eyes and a quickening drum in his chest. Slowly at first, then with swift angry turns, he reeled in the line. There was something on the end of the hook this time.

As it slowly ascended from the black waters that reflected the darkening sky above, the creature coiled and writhed around the hook. John's brow furrowed as he wound the creature in. It was a worm. But a worm unlike any creature the boy had seen before. It had a mouth like a leech. It opened and closed revealing tiny vicious teeth. The green skin oozed and slimed as it turned this way and that. It wasn't caught on the hook but rather clinging to it.

The boy was hypnotised as the horrible creature approached. He was making it get closer yet didn't want it to. As it dangled in mid-air in front of him, translucent thick liquid dripped to the river bank. The boy was repulsed yet could not look away.

He shook his head, clearing the mist that had gathered there. Not wanting, not daring, to touch it, he felt the floor and found a twig. He prodded the worm and it gripped the hook even tighter.

The boy stood and tore his eyes from the creature to scan the landscape around him. Near to the river was a well. He walked over towards it carrying the rod in two hands. He walked slowly, reverently even, like he was carrying a chalice in church. His eyes were glued to the worm, he didn't blink or flinch, his wrinkled expression was chiselled upon his face.

The well was deep and dark. John peered into it and looked back at the worm. It was circling the hook, taking angry snaps at the air. He shook the hook over the well but he already knew that the worm was not going to let go. He lowered the rod, hook first down into the darkness. Then he let go.

There was a dull plopping sound as the whole rod entered the water below. The boy shuddered. He lifted his hood over his head, turned and walked away.

The worm was now a memory and that too faded as the months slipped into years. John continued with his training and eventually became a knight. His studied hard and threw himself into honing his fighting skills. He joined the Templars and travelled east. He thought that he was doing God's work but soon saw the horrors of war. He learned much while away, but mainly about the cruelty of people. He saw his comrades slaughter the innocent and they did it all in the name of God. He knew that this wasn't God's work and decided to head back for home.

Meanwhile, back in Lambton's land a lot had happened. The worm in the well had grown. It has slithered up, up, up and out into the light. It crawled on its belly and slid towards a farm. There it entered the chicken coop and feasted on flesh and feathers then slept in the hay.

When it awoke it was larger than before. As it had grown, so had its appetite. The farmer was up and about, so the worm slid back towards the river where it silently approached some ducks sleeping on the riverbank. It devoured one whole and slept again.

The worm was now the size of a small dog. It silently slithered back to the farm where it feasted upon a sheep. Day after day it returned to the farm. Day after day it grew. The farmer found it one day busily and noisily biting its way through the belly of a pig. He had grabbed a scythe and sliced the creature in two. But, the worm joined itself back together with a terrible slurping sound. Then it turned on the farmer and ate him too.

Now that the worm had tasted human flesh, it liked that best of all. It was now the length of a field and had changed in appearance as well as size. It was a dark, emerald colour and covered in thick, fist-sized scales. An arrow-pointed tail was as wide as an ancient tree trunk. Its mouth was now a long snout that had row after row of impossibly sharp teeth. It was an engine of destruction with an appetite deeper than the well it had emerged from and a heart blacker than the depths from which it was fished.

The legless serpent slithered the Lambton's land feasting on the flesh of the people that lived there. The people fought back but were no match for the invincible foe. Even if their weapons cut the creature, it would simply heal its own wounds instantly. If any part of it was chopped away from its body, then it would rejoin in a matter of moments.

A horde of desperate survivors arrived at Lambton Castle in search of an answer. Most of the knights of the north were off fighting in the Crusades, but Lord and Lady Lambton sent word of their dire need across the country.

While they waited for a reply it was decided that the worm should be fed. A full belly would mean that it would not hunt for humans. So, each day two cows were tethered to a trough that was filled with milk. This offering was left near to sightings of the worm and each day the milk was drunk and all that was left of the cows were bones. It was working. But the people of Lambton, including the Lord and Lady, were poor. Everything they had was sold to supply food for the awful creature.

Eventually a small army arrived at the castle. These were either veterans who were recently returned from the Holy Land or rookies who were bound for battle abroad in the near future. They met at the castle and were supplied with fresh horses from the stable and newly forged weapons from the armoury. With galloping hooves that sent mud flying into the air, the fighting men raced towards the worm.

It had found its home around a hill. Its scaly body was coiled seven times around the grassy heap. It opened one eye when it saw the army approach. A low, growling sound made the earth shake and the horses panic. The knights dismounted and charged on foot. They chopped and hacked the worm to pieces. They roared with satisfaction and pointed their weapons at the sky in honour of their great, swift victory. But a terrible slurping sound filled the air. They turned and saw the worm had healed itself. They charged and hacked again. They swung their morning stars, chopped with axes and stabbed with broadswords. Each time they thought they had killed the worm there was that sound again. Flesh meeting flesh. Skin sliding onto skin. Bone crunching into bone.

Then the worm made its own attack. The tail whipped, the jaws snapped. One by one the knights were beaten, broken and bitten. One by one they were defeated.

From afar, the people of Lambton saw their only hope fall. With heads hung low they accepted that this land was no longer that of the Lambtons. This was the lair of the worm and no place for people to live. They prayed in the chapel of Lambton Castle for help from God.

'It is the devil,' the priest had told them. 'It is prophesied in the Book of Revelation that the devil will come to us in the form of a dragon. Here it is!'

It was at this time that John Lambton arrived back to his home. His ravished, blood-splattered home. When he heard all that had happened he knew it had been of his making. He had fished the worm from the river. He had cast it down a well. So, it would be he that would defeat this devil. But he also knew that he would need help.

He had heard of a Wiccan that lived on Lambton land. He knew that everyone stayed away from her. People fear what they do not understand and she was most mysterious.

Wrapped in a thick, dirty, white cloak, John Lambton knocked at the hard wooden door of her hut. It creaked noisily open but no one stood in the doorway. He waited uncertainly for a few moments and then stepped inside. Once his eyes had adjusted to the darkness he saw she was sat by the fire.

She was much younger than he expected. Much more beautiful too. He had had visions of an old crone with warts and a hooked nose, yet here was a girl with alabaster skin, raven hair and piercing eyes of emerald.

'You took your time.'

Her voice was harsh yet playful. He smiled and stepped towards her.

'Can I sit?' he asked.

She nodded curtly towards a small stool. A look of amusement flashed across her face momentarily as he struggled to sit so low upon it.

'Do you know why I'm here?'

She nodded. Her serious expression had returned.

'Aye,' she replied with a wry smile, 'and I'll help you. But, there are conditions.'

'Name them.'

She was pulling rosemary leaves from the stem and letting them fall into a small wooden bowl.

'To kill the worm,' she began, 'you must stud your armour with spear blades. You must also not fight the creature on dry land but rather stand in the river from which it came.'

John was nodding profusely.

'That's it,' she smiled. 'Do those two things and you will defeat the worm. But it has to be you. Only you can do this, John Lambton.'

He nodded some more. Then there was silence.

'And the conditions for your guidance?' he eventually asked.

Her emerald eyes looked up from the rosemary. She stopped what she as doing and looked at him intently.

'You must kill the first living thing that you see once the worm is dead.'

She let the words hang in the air for a few moments. She let them seep into him.

'Do you understand John Lambton?' she asked, insistently, 'Do you hear me?'

'I do.'

'If my conditions are not met,' she let the sinister words simmer for a while, 'then your family will be cursed for generations to come.' John stood up.

'I will do as you advise and adhere to your conditions. And I thank you.'

She chuckled. It was a light, tinkling sound. Then she ignored him and used a pestle to grind the rosemary into a powder. He turned and left her, his mind awash with thoughts of the battle ahead. A tidal wave of possible outcomes.

The armoury at first appeared deserted but John could hear the blacksmith at his forge. The rhythmic ringing of his hammer on metal counted John's footsteps as he approached. The blacksmith's black, sooted face looked up and the hammer stopped mid-air.

'Evening, sir.'

'I need something,' John began. 'If I'm to kill the worm then I need your help.'

The blacksmith nodded all the while John explained how he wanted his armour adapted.

'I'll work on it all night,' he said. 'It'll be ready by morning.'

John thanked him and headed inside the castle to tell his parents of his plans.

'The first living thing that you meet?' his father had said. 'It could be anything.'

'No,' his mother said slowly, 'we decide what it is. We control this.' The two men looked at her.

'Take a bugle and sound it out once you are victorious, my son. We shall release a hunting dog from the castle. It shall be called by the sound. When you see it. Kill it. That shall be the first living thing that you meet.'

'A glorious plan!' Lord Lambton laughed.

No sleep came for anyone that night. The steady hammering of the blacksmith's hammer ticked the night away. As the first shafts of light penetrated the cracks in the curtains, John Lambton was already up.

His parents were saddling his horse themselves and the black-smith had the spear-bladed armour laid out and ready. Wordlessly, John had his armour strapped to his body and mounted his horse. He looked down at his parents. The blacksmith turned and walked away.

'Oh John,' gasped his mother, 'we can send another.'

He shook his head.

'It's to be me.'

She handed him the bugle with tears filling her eyes.

'Good luck son.' his father said.

John flicked at the reins and the rhythmic clopping of steady hooves rattled onto the cobblestones then onto the softer terrain outside of the castle. He headed up to a trot then a gallop and made his way to the river.

The serpentine black coils were soon in sight and John guided the horse to a suitable spot where he dismounted and tethered his steed to a large tree. There was a rock jutting from the swift water. John saw that the river here was shallow. It was the perfect place for the forthcoming battle.

He waded the water and despite bring shallow the currents nearly toppled him several times. His sword was used as a walking stick, yet he nearly dropped his great helm repeatedly. Eventually he clambered up onto the large, smooth rock and steadied himself. The surface was flat and sleek. He would need to be careful not to fall when the worm came.

He scanned the land beyond. Nothing.

'Come on!' he bellowed. 'Come and get me you cowardly creature!'

He waited. He shouted again. And again.

Then there was a rumbling sound. The horse began to panic. It pulled at the reins around the trunk with such ferocity that they came loose. It galloped away, screeching in terror.

John placed his helmet upon his head. The thin-slit view revealed the worm sliding its way towards him. Its bulging eyes were focused upon him and him alone. A long, scarlet tongue flicked the air hungrily. A look of utter rage was transfixed upon the monstrous mouth. John held his sword in two hands.

'Come on!' he roared. 'Come on then!'

The worm stopped at the riverbank and coiled its tail in a circle. It reared its head up to strike. John became a statue. He readied himself to strike back.

The green, scaly head lunged and John slashed. The sword met flesh and a shower of black blood splashed all over his armour. The worm screamed in pain and fury. It slithered sideways and lashed at him with its tail. He sliced the end clean off. It plopped into the water and was whisked away by the fast-moving currents before it could join itself back together.

It gnashed at him with its teeth and John sliced, just missing its eyes. The worm lashed and gnashed repeatedly. But John's swift sword hacked off several more parts of the worm. Each one landed in the river and sped away.

The worm realised it need another plan of attack. It coiled and circled John. It wrapped itself around him, trying to crush him like some Amazonian constrictor. But as his armour was studded in spear blades it squeezed itself onto certain death. It cut itself into dozens of parts and fell dead into the river from which it came.

John was a sleek black-bloodied mess. Tatters of flesh hung from the blades on his armour. The once silver, shining steel was oily and dripping.

He staggered into the river and waded towards the bank. He collapsed then, breathless and panting. The great helm fell from his head. Fumbling for the bugle, he finally brought it to his lips and gave three short blasts.

Back at the castle Lord Lambton had paced the corridors, battlements and staircases. When he heard the bugle he gasped. Racing from the castle on foot he had his arms outstretched and was bellowing,

'My son! You did it!'

The father reached the son and beamed with pride.

'John!' Lord Lambton gasped. 'John!'

Looking up at his father with disbelieving eyes John said,

'The Wiccan! Father, the curse!'

The jubilant expression fell from Lord Lambton's face. He helped his son to his feet.

'Here comes the hound now,' he said. 'Kill it and all will be well.' John thrust his sword at the approaching lurcher. It yipped and fell to the floor.

'It is done,' Lord Lambton said, 'All will be well.'

He led his son towards the castle repeating the words again and again as if by saying them enough times then it would make it so.

'All will be well.'

But all was not well. John Lambton had defeated the worm but the Wiccan's curse came true. She would not be fooled by Lord Lambton's trickery. Nine generations of Lambtons died horrible and unnatural deaths. None died peacefully in their beds. Some died on the battlefield, one died by drowning and the last of the nine died in his carriage crossing Lambton Bridge. The curse is now lifted but the awful story of the Lambton Worm lives on in song and in story.

One Sunday morn young Lambton went
A-fishing' in the Wear;
An' catched a fish upon he's heuk,
He thowt leuk't varry queer.
But whatt'n a kind of fish it was
Young Lambton cuddent tell.
He waddn't fash te carry'd hyem,
So he hoyed it doon a well.

cho: Whisht! Lads, haad yor gobs,
An Aa'll tell ye's aall an aaful story
Whisht! Lads, haad yor gobs,
An' Aa'll tell ye 'boot the worm.

Noo Lambton felt inclined te gan
An' fight i' foreign wars.
he joined a troop o' Knights that cared
For nowther woonds nor scars,
An' off he went te Palestine
Where queer things him befel,
An' varry seun forgat aboot
The queer worm i' the well.

But the worm got fat an' growed and' growed
An' growed an aaful size;
He'd greet big teeth, a greet big gob,
An' greet big goggle eyes.
An' when at neets he craaled aboot
Te pick up bits o' news,
If he felt dry upon the road,
He milked a dozen coos.

This feorful worm wad often feed
On caalves an' lambs an' sheep,
An' swally little barins alive
When they laid doon te sleep.
An' when he'd eaten aall he cud
An' he had had he's fill,
He craaled away an' lapped he's tail
Seven times roond Pensher Hill.

The news of this myest aaful worm
An' his queer gannins on
Seun crossed the seas, gat te the ears

Ov brave and' bowld Sor John.
So hyem he cam an' catched the beast
An' cut 'im in twe haalves,
An' that seun stopped he's eatin' bairns,
An' sheep an' lambs and caalves.

So noo ye knaa hoo aall the foaks
On byeth sides ov the Wear
Lost lots o' sheep an' lots o' sleep
An' leeved i' mortal feor.
So let's hev one te brave Sor John
That kept the bairns frae harm,
Saved coos an' caalves by myekin' haalves
O' the famis Lambton Worm.

Final Chorus

Noo lads, Aa'll haad me gob,
That's aall Aa knaa aboot the story
Ov Sor John's clivvor job
Wi' the aaful Lambton Worm.

BIBLIOGRAPHY

Brockie, W., *Legends and Superstitions of the County of Durham* (Williams 1886)

Crawhall, J., *History of James Allan, the Celebrated Northumberland Piper* (Zaehnsdorf Ltd 2015)

Grice, F., *Folk Tales of the North Country* (Thomas Nelson and Sons Ltd 1944)

Reader's Digest, *Folklore, Myths and Legends of Britain* (Reader's Digest 1977)

Sharp, C., *The Bishoprick Garland, A Collection of Legends, Songs and Ballads of the County of Durham* (Nichols, Baldwin and Cradock 1834)

Westwood, J. and Simpson J., *The Lore of the Land, A Guide to England's Legends* (Penguin Reference 2005)

ABOUT THE AUTHOR

ADAM BUSHNELL was previously teacher and has worked as a storyteller since 2004. He is a published author of both fiction and academia and is now a visiting author working in the UK and internationally, delivering writing workshops and staff training. He is the author of eleven books of fiction and two academic books for teachers on how to help children write creatively.

www.adambushnell.co.uk

Society *for*
Storytelling

Since 1993, the Society for Storytelling has championed the art of oral storytelling and the benefits it can provide – such as improving memory more than rote learning, promoting healing by stimulating the release of neuropeptides, or simply great entertainment! Storytellers, enthusiasts and academics support and are supported by this registered charity to ensure the art is nurtured and developed throughout the UK.

Many activities of the Society are available to all, such as locating storytellers on the Society website, taking part in our annual National Storytelling Week at the start of every February, purchasing our quarterly magazine *Storylines*, or attending our Annual Gathering – a chance to revel in engaging performances, inspiring workshops, and the company of like-minded people.

You can also become a member of the Society to support the work we do. In return, you receive free access to *Storylines*, discounted tickets to the Annual Gathering and other story-telling events, the opportunity to join our mentorship scheme for new storytellers, and more. Among our great deals for members is a 30% discount off titles in the *Folk Tales* series from The History Press website.

For more information, including how to join, please visit

www.sfs.org.uk